Dr Mil
EATI

Dr Mike Smith is a sp
and President of the Association of —
Doctors. He was the Chief Medical Officer of the
Family Planning Association 1970–75 and their
Honorary Medical Adviser 1975–90. He is an elected
member of the FPA's National Executive Committee, a
member of the Pet Health Council and a member of
the advisory panel of the National Food Safety
Advisory Centre. For many years he has been a 'resi-
dent' expert guest on BBC Radio 2's *Jimmy Young
Show*, LBC's *Nightline* and the medical columnist/edi-
tor for *Woman's Own*. Between 1980 and 1984 he pre-
sented BBC1's health series *Looking Good, Feeling Fit*
and from 1988–90 he was the expert guest on SKY
TV's *Sky by Day*. In April 1991 he was voted the TV
and Radio Doctors' 'Expert's Expert' in the *Observer*
magazine's series.

As well as the Postbag series, he is also the author of
Birth Control, *How to Save Your Child's Life*, *A New
Dictionary of Symptoms*, *Dr Mike Smith's Handbook of
Over-the-Counter Medicines*, *Dr Mike Smith's Handbook
of Prescription Medicines* and *Dr Mike Smith's First Aid
Handbook* (to be published May 1994).

Dr Mil
EATI

Dr Mike Smith is a s[
and President of the Association of ...
Doctors. He was the Chief Medical Officer of the
Family Planning Association 1970–75 and their
Honorary Medical Adviser 1975–90. He is an elected
member of the FPA's National Executive Committee, a
member of the Pet Health Council and a member of
the advisory panel of the National Food Safety
Advisory Centre. For many years he has been a 'resi-
dent' expert guest on BBC Radio 2's *Jimmy Young
Show*, LBC's *Nightline* and the medical columnist/edi-
tor for *Woman's Own*. Between 1980 and 1984 he pre-
sented BBC1's health series *Looking Good, Feeling Fit*
and from 1988–90 he was the expert guest on SKY
TV's *Sky by Day*. In April 1991 he was voted the TV
and Radio Doctors' 'Expert's Expert' in the *Observer*
magazine's series.

As well as the Postbag series, he is also the author of
*Birth Control, How to Save Your Child's Life, A New
Dictionary of Symptoms, Dr Mike Smith's Handbook of
Over-the-Counter Medicines, Dr Mike Smith's Handbook
of Prescription Medicines* and *Dr Mike Smith's First Aid
Handbook* (to be published May 1994).

Also in Dr Mike Smith's Postbag series

Arthritis
Back Pain
Stress
HRT
Migraine
Allergies
Skin Problems

DR MIKE SMITH'S

POSTBAG

EATING DISORDERS

WITH SHARRON KERR

KYLE CATHIE LIMITED

First published in Great Britain in 1994 by
Kyle Cathie Limited
7/8 Hatherley Street, London SW1P 2QT

ISBN 1 85626 121 2

A Cataloguing in Publication record for this title is
available from the British Library.

Typeset by Heronwood Press, Medstead, Hampshire
Printed by Cox & Wyman Ltd, Reading

CONTENTS

INTRODUCTION

The pressure to be slim and to strive for 'perfection' comes from a variety of sources and pressurizes men and women from all walks of life, in all manner of situations. Women's magazines, which may confront the problems about eating disorders head-on with straight-talking features, are sometimes the worst offenders in terms of portraying the body beautiful as every woman's unquestionable desire. But it doesn't stop there . . .

Just imagine it – a young girl at ballet school. Day after day she's forced to confront her body image – not through any fault of her own but simply because she trains in mirrored rooms dressed in a tight-fitting leotard. Even if she is happy with her body, the external pressures are ever-present. Who has ever seen an overweight cast dancing *Swan Lake*? And there's even pressure regarding her height: too fat or too tall, and that's the end of her career.

Ballet students are far from the only ones at risk, however. According to the Royal College of Psychiatrists, one in every hundred secondary school girls has full-blown anorexia, two in every hundred women aged fifteen to forty-five have bulimia.

In countries where food is scarce people hold fatness in esteem and value it as a sign of beauty and wealth. And in these societies, not surprisingly, eating disorders are not very common. But in Western civilization the disorders are very common indeed and seem to be on the increase. The Princess of Wales – who is herself alleged to have suffered from bulimia – highlighted the plight of sufferers in a speech to the International Conference on Eating Disorders 93. She pointed out that by focusing their energies on controlling their bodies, these people had found a refuge from facing the more painful issues at the centre of their lives: '"A way of coping", albeit destructively and pointlessly, but a way of coping with a situation they were finding unbearable. An expression of how they felt about themselves and the life they were living.'

There are many theories as to why eating problems are on the increase, though some suggest that the disorders have always been with us but just weren't talked about. Others argue that the pressures of modern living have meant that more and more people are turning to food abuse as a form of coping. I believe we now expect more out of life – in the developing world (as in Britain 150 years ago) you are successful if you get enough to eat and avoid disease; nowadays you've 'failed' if that's all you can do.

This suggestion seems to be supported by a leading psychiatrist, Professor Hubert Lacey, who recently warned that modern pressures on women to rise in their careers and yet be a perfect wife and mother are leading to self-destruction. Apparently the number of women with bulimia who have also harmed themselves in other ways has risen by three times. We're talking here of women who not only binge on food then purge themselves by vomiting or taking laxatives, but women who are more frequently using drugs and alcohol as part of their self-abuse. Professor Lacey told the annual conference of the Royal College of Psychiatrists that women are expected to achieve high standards academically, succeed at work and at home without the usual assertiveness shown by men. His opinion is that some bulimics turn that assertiveness in on themselves.

What is generally agreed upon is that very often people with eating disorders have had a problem childhood. Eating disorders and troubled childhoods are linked because this type of upbringing is highly likely to have led to the development of very low self-esteem.

Unless you have suffered from it, it is very difficult to imagine the problems a total lack of self-esteem can cause, and difficult to understand how it can lead to over-dependence on others to provide a sense of emotional security and self-value. In reality it's only the sufferer who can give herself or himself those values – because believing that other people will always satisfy your emotional needs will doubtlessly lead to disappointment.

Low self-esteem can create all sorts of problems in later life. For one thing it is linked with a lack of assertiveness. It's not easy to say what we want if we feel we're not worth it. Sufferers need to accept that something going wrong is forgivable or understandable or totally out of their control, not a sign of incompetence.

Another worrying aspect is the growing number of children who seem to be developing eating disorders. Could it be that here again the media, fashion industry, advertisers and even the music business are to blame? When young girls' role models are stars like Kylie Minogue or Madonna or the new fashionable waif-like models is it any wonder that they are 'brainwashed' into thinking this is how young women are supposed to look? That if they are slightly above what they regard as a longed-for weight or longed-for shape they start to diet as young as eleven, twelve or thirteen? These girls sadly fail to realize that the fashion and film industry loves using models with physiques that are virtually unobtainable for most females. And, of course, dieting at such a young age can lead to all sorts of additional problems at a time when it's already hard enough to deal with puberty and adolescence.

Women are ten times more likely to suffer from eating disorders than men. Again we don't know why that is, though the obvious gender differences, such as hormones, and the faster changing roles of women must, in my opinion, have a lot to do with it. However, a recent Mori survey revealed that one in three men diet because they are concerned about their body image, and that six out of ten believe that a change in shape would make them more attractive to the opposite sex. According to psychiatrists, this trend shows that men too could, more commonly than at present, fall victim to eating disorders.

Many counsellors believe that the underlying reasons for men developing eating disorders are the same as for women, although it is suggested that for some men the equivalent of an eating disorder is an overwhelming obsession with exercise routines and pumping iron. They are drawn into the discipline of exercise because they want to have control over some aspect of their life or they want to reinforce their self-esteem. They may also believe that through exercise they can become more attractive to the opposite sex.

It has to be said that for both men and women eating disorders are the result of emotional disturbances that are expressed through that person's behaviour. But a fundamental problem is, as I've said, that shape and image now dominate our culture. You only have to think of an Old Master's nudes, or those of the Impressionists to notice how the concept of a beautiful woman's shape has become 'downsized'.

Walk into any newsagents and there you'll find rows of magazines with cover lines shouting phrases like *Lose weight and find the man of your dreams*; *New ways for slimmer hips and thighs*; *Yes, you too can look like a cover girl*. The variations on the theme of thin equals success, equals sex, equals happiness, are endless. Go shopping and the subconscious mental pounding continues. Every clothes shop window seems full of dummies which are a trim size 8 or 10. It seems to me you never see a size 16 shop dummy. So what messages are being sent to the shopper? To be normal and acceptable you need to be slim. If only everyone would stop and think, it's what you *are* that matters, not what you look like.

Recently eating disorders have attracted plenty of media attention. Hopefully this in turn will lead to better awareness of the problem and a greater under-standing of it. But, despite this current attention, the disorders continue to affect large numbers of women, and, of course, men. Many experts consider that eating disorders are misunderstood. In this book I hope to clear up this misunderstanding by explaining what eat-ing disorders are, what can be done to help and where you can go to find this help.

I feel that with more information on the problem, sufferers will get the sympathy and understanding they deserve. We need to understand that an eating disorder isn't a question of vanity. And the sooner there is greater awareness, the sooner sufferers can be helped.

1: SOME COMMON CONCERNS ABOUT THE EFFECTS OF FOOD

When we talk about eating disorders, we usually mean anorexia, bulimia, compulsive eating and obesity. However I know from my postbag that there are other areas about food and its effects on the human body that concern people. The most common questions are what is food intolerance, what is food phobia and what is a food fad?

FOOD INTOLERANCE

A food intolerance may produce puzzling symptoms such as headaches, diarrhoea, vomiting or bloating – virtually anything, in fact, as symptoms differ enormously between sufferers.

People are generally rather confused about the differences between an allergy and an intolerance (sometimes also called a sensitivity). The difference is that for a definite allergy to be diagnosed, the presence of a 'hostile' chemical in the body – called an antibody – can usually be confirmed, or at least a change in the blood's make-up that is recognized as being associated with an allergy. That is to say, there will usually be objective evidence of a definite allergy that is not subject solely to the patient's feelings about it. If there is this evidence, then that food will need to be avoided since desensitizing treatments have not proved effective and have largely been abandoned.

For an intolerance, the indicators are less clear. The usual symptoms are being sick or feeling faint soon after the offending food is eaten. Some sufferers will feel nauseous or may even be sick at the *thought* of a wide range of foods, without actually eating them. This could, therefore, be due to an unconsious aversion to the thought of the food rather than anything physical. These symptoms could pass in time or with a change in circumstance, or even with psychotherapy, if the effects of the intolerance warrant such help.

Confusion over these differences could be one of the reasons why food intolerance problems are not discovered as early as they might be. As the symptoms are often triggered by many natural items in the patient's diet the majority of doctors and scientists are unable to establish the cause. As a result, a different specialist area has evolved, often known as clinical ecology. This basically involves a series of observations of people's symptoms and feelings towards what are generally seen as common-or-garden foodstuffs, and then recommending that these foods are avoided. As long as this treatment doesn't alter the patient's diet so that they are no longer receiving the food their body needs, then that's fine.

People often ask me what causes food intolerance and the honest answer is, nobody really knows. Some clinical ecologists think that it is due to a trigger food and leakage from the sufferer's alimentary canal. Although the meaning of this is less than clear – since it's a theory that has not been proved – I think what is meant is that whole food particles that are digesting in the stomach and bowel are thought to leak somehow through the walls in minuscule amounts and trigger an intolerance, provoking the symptoms. Normally, only digested food particles are able to pass through the walls, so the suggestion is that if you avoid that particular food you will avoid the symptoms. This need not provoke a true allergy and may not be a problem that lasts for ever.

Many, if not most, traditional doctors and specialists do not recognize the specialty of clinical ecology. They argue that the benefits claimed by someone treated by such methods are usually more related to the care and attention paid to them by the therapist. The beneficial effect of a caring professional has long been recognized as 'the bedside manner'.

What is undoubtedly true is that a small number of people do suffer from very distressing symptoms, for which no medical cause can be found. And, for some of these sufferers, a practitioner who is well-versed in 'elimination diets' can establish a relationship between certain foods and the symptoms – and will continue to do so whatever the cynical scientists may say! At the start the elimination diet is often restricted to foods which are considered to be safe – for example, pears, lamb and bottled water. Then, gradually, other components of the usual diet are added one at a time until the sufferer feels the symptoms returning (or getting worse if they've been there all along).

Based on these observations a diet is suggested to the sufferer, which avoids all the foods found to cause the symptoms. With luck, there won't be too many of these foods, and the sufferer will be able to eat a well-balanced and varied diet while remaining symptom-free.

I think it's fair to say that the practice of clinical ecology, as I've described, is more an art than a science, but as long as it makes the sufferer feel better and eliminates most or all of the symptoms then that's fine.

When clinical ecology is their main curative activity, practitioners have to charge private fees. This type of treatment is not a specialty recognized within the NHS, although many family doctors and hospital consultants will sometimes use exclusion diets as part of the state health service.

FOOD PHOBIAS AND FADS

Anxiety, when it's not overwhelming, is called worry and this state of mind is likely to stay with us until the problem is sorted out. When a threat is more immediate and feels like a burden hanging over us, this is fear. When fear takes a hold it's called a phobia. This fear is often the basis of a food fad, when the sufferer will only – *can only* – eat certain foods or they will be physically sick.

Food fads are not at all uncommon in children. I remember (and my mother used to remind me constantly) that in early childhood I went through a phase of eating virtually nothing except boiled potatoes and a well-known brand of salad cream. Although I loved her dearly, and she was a very good mum, I realized in later years that cooking was not an activity in which she excelled, to put it at its kindest! When I later lived away from home, I started to eat a normal diet within a matter of days! The purpose of this personal aside is to point out that children, in particular, may take against certain tastes that grown-ups consider to be perfectly good and nutritious.

But if food fads persist in a dramatic way they are sometimes due to a direct and definite physical intolerance – to oysters, for example, or pork. The sufferer will normally be completely well but if they eat the food, even without realizing it (if it was in a fish pie or a stew, for example), they vomit it all back, within a matter of minutes in the most serious cases.

However, there will also be those who either consciously or unconsciously suffer from a 'poison' phobia. This will sometimes take the form of being able to eat only 'plain' food – that is, food untouched by spices or sauces of any kind. The basis for this fear is that spices and sauces can more readily hide the taste of a poison.

It isn't rational and the person concerned may have even forgotten the reason they started avoiding spices and sauces in the first place!

When a diagnosed food fad is resulting in real problems, such as causing the sufferer to eat such an abnormal diet that there are nutritional deficiencies, then sensitive counselling or psychotherapy are the favoured treatments. But many mild food fads need not cause nutrition problems and may remain throughout a sufferer's life without the need for treatment, other than attention to what they can and cannot eat.

There will, of course, simply be perfectly healthy people who just don't like the taste of certain foods, perhaps because they were made to eat them as a child and ever since the mere thought of the taste makes them nauseous.

Did my childhood food fad last? No. Not only am I always planning to do something about being a stone overweight (next week!) but I have not yet come across a food which I positively dislike.

2: ANOREXIA NERVOSA

WHAT IS ANOREXIA?

I'm sure there can't be many of us who at some time or another haven't considered ourselves too fat and have wanted a healthier or slimmer body. And, consequently, who hasn't tried some form of diet, be it calorie-controlled or low-fat, high-fibre or fruit-and-vegetables only?

Most dieters keep within reasonable limits, or only diet for the run-up to their summer holiday, or don't have the will-power to diet for longer than a couple of weeks. These people don't usually endanger their health and the dieting doesn't become an obsession. More importantly, most dieters are not using food and nourishment as a means of attacking themselves and as a way of coping with life. They don't believe that they are failures who need to gain a sense of achievement by losing lots of weight. Most people diet for one motive only – to lose weight.

But those who diet because they are literally terrified of being fat (mainly young girls) become abnormally obsessed with controlling their intake of food and every detail of it and may go on to develop anorexia nervosa.

'Anorexia nervosa' actually means, in its simplest sense, the loss of appetite for nervous reasons. Yet the term in this case is unsuitable because the sufferer is, in reality, continually hungry. Everybody needs to eat in order to live, and eating is a basic instinct. So in the case of an anorexic the appetite has, in fact, been far from lost. What the sufferer *has* lost is any ability to let themselves satisfy this hunger. Their life becomes one long process of denial – denying themselves food, denying they have a problem, denying they are emaciated, denying help.

We assume it's a recent phenomenon – totally based on modern 'image' needs – but I'm not sure about that. Nowadays, more than ever before, we are able to diagnose, count and record accurately what ails us. Computers allow us to see trends in disease. Before they were around it's probable that the findings, if anorexia was being diagnosed, weren't shared with others but kept in the records of the individual therapist. So the disease's *national importance* wasn't recognized.

Sufferers believe themselves to be fat when in reality they are extremely thin. They continue to diet, sometimes surviving on the tiniest amounts of food – a carrot one day, an apple or a cereal bar the next. They become suspicious of food that tastes good, suspecting someone of secretly adding sugar to a piece of fruit, say, and therefore boosting calorie intake. They will consider even these tiny amounts too much and some will even resort to self-induced vomiting or take laxatives as a way of ridding the body of these calories.

There is general agreement that out of all the eating disorders, anorexia is potentially the most dangerous – it is very often life-threatening and even when less serious can lead to unpleasant side-effects. It's been described as a slow form of suicide, though some experts would disagree with this because eating disorders are more a way of coping with life than of wanting to die. But no matter how it's described, anorexia is a sad and dangerous condition. Sufferers should seek help as soon as they are able.

The Eating Disorders Association estimates that each year as many as one hundred sufferers die because of anorexia. As the association points out, though this may seem a small number eating disorders have one of the highest mortality rates of all psychiatric illnesses. Deaths occur in young women or men who without the condition could have been leading healthy and fulfilled lives.

To appreciate the seriousness of the disorder, and to understand that it isn't a slimming disease or the result of teenage vanity, you need to realize that anorexia is mainly about obtaining a degree of control when a sufferer believes his or her life is quite out of control. It's not about just being stubborn and not wanting to eat, it's far more complex than that.

For the anorexic, life is a constant battle to restrain her appetite in order to control her weight and shape. Whereas to an onlooker the sufferer often looks emaciated, like a victim of a concentration camp with bones protruding from her flesh, the sufferer still considers herself fat. The thinner she becomes the thinner she longs to be, and so the dieting continues. It's fairly common for a sufferer to believe – in her distorted view of the world – that she is up to 50 per cent fatter than she actually is. She sets herself a target weight, but once she's reached that target, she will set herself another, one that is even lower and even more damaging to her health. It's a downward spiral she finds hard to resist. These are the crucial features of anorexia – a distorted body image and a dreaded fear of weight gain.

That's why every pound lost is seen as a victory, and a pound gained can drive the victim to the depths of despair. Unfortunately many young women, and men, start to diet when they are not overweight. This poses an even greater risk to their health and development. But even if they are overweight, by reducing their intake of food to such extremes – as I've said, some sufferers eat little more than an apple and a cream cracker a day – weight can very quickly drop to well below the norm for their age and height.

The consequences of such a strict regime, as you can imagine, are quite serious. At a certain point this weight loss will cause her periods to stop (or, if not yet established, fail to start) and her developing body will begin to revert to its pre-pubescent shape. If dieting starts before the end of puberty she may not even develop pubic hair or breasts – outward signs of being an adult woman. It seems that many anorexics wish, perhaps subconsciously, to remain childlike, fearing the responsibilities and relationships – especially the sexual ones – of adulthood. This in turn leads to further problems. By 'opting out' of maturity the sufferer doesn't deal with the everyday problems of growing up.

I rarely get letters from sufferers themselves. They don't seek help or information. But I do get letters from parents, relatives or friends, deeply worried and concerned about what they can do. Regrettably, unlike most conditions, there isn't a box of pills or an operation that can bring about a cure.

WHO IS LIKELY TO DEVELOP ANOREXIA?

There's no simple answer to this because anorexia isn't a simple disorder, as I've already hinted. Each case is different. The events and pressures that cause someone to develop anorexia are extremely complex and will vary with each individual. However one thing is certain, parents, partners and relatives should not always blame themselves, believing that their past actions have brought on the disorders (although I know that is easier said than done when family relationship problems may have triggered the condition).

As I've said, there are no rigid rules about who will develop anorexia – sufferers can be affected in childhood or middle age, or even older, as unlikely as that may seem. Experts agree that adolescent girls are the most likely age group to be affected and the average age for anorexia to appear is eighteen. It could be that as many as one in every 200 girls aged between sixteen and eighteen is affected. According to the Royal College of Psychiatrists, one in every 150 fifteen-year-old girls has anorexia. These figures are alarming. Some figures suggest that it's ten times more common in girls than boys, while others suggest that one in every twenty sufferers will be male.

Although the circumstances that trigger anorexia vary with each individual, and may or may not be fairly straightforward, you can make general assumptions about the type of person likely to suffer. The young girl, for instance, is usually intelligent, sensitive and lacking in self-confidence, with very low self-esteem. Yet she may have ambitions and high expectations of her own. And she may feel, albeit wrongly, that she never quite lives up to the expectations of her parents. She can feel that she has no real value as a person and that she is only valuable in her parents' eyes when she has been successful at school, for instance. She may have been an easy child – always playing the part of the good girl, always anxious to please.

Interestingly, anorexia nervosa is thought to be more common in middle- and upper-class families. One assumption is that in these families there is far more pressure to succeed, which in turn depends upon performing and keeping up appearances – image again. Again, it's only a suggestion, since sufferers can come from a variety of backgrounds – as I said, there are no hard and fast rules.

Sometimes other members of the family have had similar symptoms. This suggests that there may be some common pressures within the family bringing them about. Often there is long-standing tension within the family, anxieties about school or some upset in stability, such as moving house or a father losing his job, which makes the child more vulnerable. There could be sibling rivalry or even bullying at school.

Even genes have been implicated. A recent report in the *Journal of Psychological Medicine*, compiled by a team based at the Institute of Psychiatry in London and led by Dr Rutherford, put forward evidence for such a link. The team recruited 246 pairs of twins, ninety-nine of them identical and thus sharing exactly the same genetic blueprint. Each was given the Eating Attitudes Test and Eating Disorder Inventory, psychological profiling questionnaires devised about ten years ago to research eating disorders. The results showed the pattern of some traits, such as unhappiness about appearance, that have been linked to anorexia. Dr Rutherford and her colleagues found that body dissatisfaction and a desire for thinness were more common among identical twins than ordinary twins – suggesting a genetic influence (all other factors having been covered by the sophisticated techniques).

The team converted its findings into a heritability factor of zero – no genetic influence at all – to 100 per cent – complete genetic determination. Body dissatisfaction was found to have the highest heritability of 52 per cent – suggesting that genes are actually more important than environment in determining this trait.

Anorexia becomes a way of providing security – control over one aspect of the victim's life. For some sufferers it could be the first time they have 'taken control' – from now on, only *they* are in charge of what they eat and what they look like. Dieting can exemplify control and a sense of achievement – haven't you ever been pleased with yourself and felt a sense of achievement when you've lost a couple of pounds? The anorexic takes this control and sense of achievement to extremes.

Anorexia can be triggered by stress or a traumatic event – sexual abuse, the break up of a relationship, parents getting divorced, a bereavement or just as a result of the social pressures piled on to women these days to be carers and homekeepers, to be successful academically while at the same time attractive and slim. Or it could be that adolescence is so confusing the sufferer just doesn't know how to behave in the new 'adult' world, or at a later age, say around eighteen, when teenagers usually leave home, they may be frightened of leading their own fully independent life. All the while, the anorexic may not even be consciously aware of what she is doing, she just has a compulsion to do it without knowing why. She may be determined not to give in to her appetite, especially in front of other people.

Sadly, anorexia seems to be affecting children at a younger and younger age, with some starting to diet just as they are entering puberty. Sometimes this can be the result of bullying at school, especially when it involves name-calling such as 'Fatty', 'Fatso' or variations on that theme. Some children deny themselves food to express their feelings: eating food someone has prepared for you can give pleasure to the person who cooked it, so rejecting it can cause hurt. It's in this way that a child may reject food within the family – it's the only way they feel they will get any attention or have any influence. *They* feel hurt so they want to hurt back.

WARNING SIGNS AND PHYSICAL SYMPTOMS

I'm often asked about the warning signs parents should look out for. Well, if your daughter or relative, or friend for that matter, begins to lose a lot of weight that is your first cause for concern – as a rough guide, once it goes down more than seven pounds below the average weight for their height coupled with an apparent obsession for counting calories. Some sufferers even leave a crumb of bread on a plate for fear of the calories it could add to their daily intake.

The person may seem to be eating a large quantity of food – but when the diet is examined more closely it's not unusual to find that the sufferer is eating large quantities of very low-calorie foods – tomatoes, celery, lettuce, apples, et cetera.

Other signs to watch for are if she becomes terrified of putting on any weight, weighs herself daily, is secretive about what she eats (possibly resorting to large doses of laxatives, or self-induced vomiting to rid herself of unwanted food) and if she begins to develop obsessive rituals which seem to take for ever to carry out (such as cutting a piece of toast into tiny pieces and eating each bit very slowly, or slicing a carrot very thinly). A sufferer is often obsessional about her schoolwork, will set herself rigid routines and timetables, and will exercise to extremes – another way to rid the body of calories.

In fact, she may suddenly become obsessed by exercise routines. She'll want to exercise as much as possible to burn up the calories that she can't bear to keep. Exercise can even include walking up and down while watching the television because sitting down wouldn't burn up enough calories. Some sufferers take slimming pills to help keep their desire to eat under strict control.

A sufferer will probably complain of feeling cold even in summer due to poor circulation and because of this may develop a downy covering of hair all over her body. As a result of feeling so cold it could be that she will begin to wear more layers of clothing than is normal.

Be concerned if she refuses to eat with the family while taking a great deal of interest in buying and preparing food for them. You may notice food that she was supposed to be taking to school or work secreted away somewhere for later undetectable disposal. If you do notice any warning signs, please seek help as soon as you can.

People ask me too about the physical symptoms of anorexia and the health risks. Common physical symptoms of anorexia are akin to symptoms resulting from starvation: extreme constipation accompanied by pain and discomfort in the abdomen, dizzy spells and, in rare instances, nutritional deficiencies – especially of protein – causing swelling of the ankles of the kind seen in starvation areas. The sufferer may find sleeping difficult and begin to suffer from insomnia. Or she may become hyperactive. She may also be more susceptible to infections.

Unfortunately, anorexia isn't without its long-term effects. One result of such poor nutrition can be osteoporosis, a thinning of the bones – the bones become brittle and cannot withstand the wear and tear of everyday activities and break easily. Indeed, osteoporosis sufferers who fracture a hip often believe a fall has caused it when, in fact, it's more likely that the weight of the body alone was enough to bring about the fracture, which then caused them to stumble.

Another very sad consequence is sterility. This usually returns to normal when the anorexia comes to an end but is, nevertheless, a consequence that can make a sufferer very bitter should they have to delay their family until later fertile years. Age alone will make it more difficult to conceive – so the sufferer may still not be able to have a baby although nothing can be found to be wrong with either her or her partner.

Severe depression can result. Depression is a common

medical condition, often described as a continuing feeling of despondency, despair and sadness. Symptoms can also include sleep disturbances, lethargy and difficulty in concentrating, sudden mood swings, thoughts of suicide, and generally feeling useless, inadequate and without hope. The sex drive can be affected, too. It's generally accepted that depression is common in anorexia, with as many as half of all cases affected by it to some degree.

Gangrene is another awful side-effect of extreme anorexia. This can lead to decay of the fingers, toes, limbs or other parts of the body because the blood supply is halted as a result of faulty circulation.

TREATMENT

Anorexia must always be taken seriously. The sufferer is usually the last person to admit there is a problem or ask for help, but if the disease becomes established it can be life-threatening. Though she sees herself wasting away, the sufferer is quite unable to stop herself. The sooner professional help is obtained, the greater the chance of recovery – although treatment may take up to two years.

The outlook for recovery is not totally black. Figures show that on average four out of ten patients will get better after an average illness of five years. Sadly, as many as two in ten sufferers die within twenty years of first developing the condition. It's thought that half of these deaths are the result of suicide.

It is hard for people to accept that anorexia nervosa isn't about a person trying to die by starvation. It's much more about dependence and the will to be totally in control of life. Part of the treatment, therefore, is for the sufferer to learn to accept their weaknesses and failures and recognize their good points. Treatment will of course include weight gain, but the patient will also need to be reassured that she will only be required to put on enough weight for her to become healthy. She won't be required to become 'fat', in its true sense of the word.

So, the first thing to do when seeking treatment for anorexia is to visit your GP. (For families concerned about a loved one who won't accept help, see pages 81–87.) You'll need to discuss with him or her what treatment is available in your area and decide what will be appropriate. There are also many private clinics which deal with eating disorders, and you can find out details of them from the Eating Disorders Association (address on page 111).

If you're terribly nervous about seeing your GP it may help to take with you some notes on the things you want to discuss. No matter how rushed your doctor may seem, it's still important to make the most of the time you've got with him or her. So there's absolutely no harm in preparing yourself mentally for a visit, in case you feel nervous or rushed once you're inside the surgery and forget to mention one of your symptoms or fears.

I know it's an easy thing to say, but don't allow yourself to be intimidated by medical staff. And this goes for psychiatric staff, as well as counsellors. If you don't understand what you're being told, make sure they realize this and ask for it to be explained more slowly or more simply. You needn't feel embarrassed or stupid – you certainly won't be the first person they've seen who's had difficulty grasping all the facts. And you won't be the last, either!

If you're worried about something in particular, make sure you ask questions about it. Very often re-assurance is all you need and there's nothing worse than anxiety stemming from ignorance.

And a note here for younger sufferers who might not want to visit their GP because he or she has known them for many years: you are perfectly entitled to change your doctor. In fact, you can change your doctor without even giving a reason. When you've decided on a new doctor, go along to the practice, preferably with your medical card, and ask whether or not you can be put on that GP's list.

Your GP may refer you to a psychiatrist. These days it's not unusual for people to seek the help of psychiatry. According to the Mental Health Foundation – Britain's leading grant-making charity concerned with promoting and encouraging research and community care projects in the field of mental health and disorder – it's thought that one man in five and one woman in four will visit a psychiatrist at some time in their lives. Eating disorders are one of the most common mental conditions for referral to psychiatrists.

Unfortunately, there is still a great deal of stigma attached to visiting a psychiatrist, but this *is* changing. Seeing a psychiatrist is now becoming much the same as seeing any other specialist. And as the foundation points out, a good psychiatrist may have insights into a situation that come from long training and experience and from being alert to all the possibilities. The psychiatrist needs information to do this, which is why assessment involves many questions. So it's important that you answer the questions truthfully. Of course, you're not *obliged* to co-operate, but by helping the psychiatrist he or she will in turn be able to help you more easily. Sometimes your psychiatrist may need to interview relatives in order to build up a picture of what sort of person you are and what stresses and strains you have been under. But remember, if there are areas of your life you don't want your family to know about, the psychiatrist has to respect your wishes.

I know from experience that people don't always realize the extensive training psychiatrists undergo: firstly qualifying as ordinary medical doctors (which takes five or six years) then undertaking a further six years or so of psychiatry training.

Your GP may also suggest psychotherapy. This therapy may include your whole family and aims to discover the reasons and emotions that caused you to turn to anorexia. It is not enough to regain weight if you will then return to the situation that made you 'need' the illness. The psychotherapist will try to provide insights and resolve the underlying problems in order to avoid a relapse.

Being severely underweight can affect a person's reasoning abilities (as well as many other systems in the body) so before any psychotherapy can be effective the sufferer must first reach a reasonable weight – which in severe cases is often best achieved in hospital.

Seeking professional help from a psychotherapist or trained counsellor is not an act of weakness, but one of strength. This is particularly true of psychotherapy, which normally requires the person to take 'a step into the dark' and investigate their unhappiness and dissatisfaction with life.

Unfortunately, the stigma about this kind of help may lead the sufferer instead to adopt an 'I can cope' attitude. And a person who does pluck up the courage to seek help may even find they encounter hostility or teasing from friends and relatives who are simply scared of the idea of psychotherapy or counselling. This situation is not helped by the fact that Britain has no official legislation for either psychotherapy or for counselling, so anyone can call themselves a counsellor or psychotherapist and sell their services to clients. I was once chatting to a waiter in a restaurant who said, 'I'm only doing this part-time now, because I've set up as a psychotherapist.' And he had about sixteen patients!

It is vital, therefore, to check the counsellor's qualifications.

Counselling and psychotherapy are not very comfortable activities. They involve talking about issues and feelings that make us miserable or distressed. Repressing our problems can seem easier than examining them, as reliving painful emotions can add to the trauma. But perhaps we should view the process as an opportunity to take certain risks that we shy away from in our everyday lives. It enables us to examine and contemplate, in a secure and confidential environment, why we – and others, too – disapprove of certain thoughts, emotions and ideas.

Remember, though, that with all therapy, recovery requires time, patience, constant reassurance and a unified approach from all concerned. However, with skilled help, this can usually be achieved.

As with so many conditions, the cure for anorexia depends upon the individual rather than medicine or an operation. Addiction to alcohol, drugs or cigarettes is rarely overcome until the sufferer fully understands that they have a problem which is simply not going to go away. If we only knew how that point of realization can be achieved we'd have the answer to the whole problem.

There are, of course, different approaches to treatment. If your weight has fallen to a dangerous level you may be advised to spend time in hospital. Here you will get the chance to have your nutrition and diet monitored while being given the opportunity to talk to professionals.

In extreme cases, it is, at best, emotionally draining for doctors and nurses to see a young life slipping away when that life could be saved by giving nutrients through a tube into the stomach or a vein, but there is a general agreement amongst doctors that they will not carry out this procedure when it is against the wishes of the patient. However, at this point, as I've said, the suf-ferer is not entirely rational so who's to decide what's the best thing to do in the circumstances?

Some hospitals offer individual psychotherapy. A 'family approach' can be offered involving all family members. Sometimes a hostel place will be offered after a spell in hospital, or there could be out-patient counsel-ling. In the past there was a tendency to treat anorexia sufferers in hospital, but now it is becoming common to treat them as out-patients, provided they have not lost too much weight and their lives are not in any danger.

The vital thing to understand about treating anorexia is that it can only be really dealt with by sorting out the *underlying problems* – as I explained earlier, the eating disorder is the sufferer's way of dealing with her prob-lems. The disorder isn't a disease in itself.

CASE STUDY: WENDY

Wendy, a twenty-year-old nursing auxiliary hoping to start training as a nurse, is living proof that recovery from anorexia can be achieved. She's five feet two inch-es tall and at her lowest point weighed only five stones.

> I first developed anorexia in 1990. I was never overweight to start with. I was ill with glandular fever and lost weight just through being ill – I must have lost about six pounds. I just went off food completely for about three weeks because of my swollen glands. I never gained weight again after that.
>
> I liked the way I was when I had lost this weight. I looked slim – I'd visibly lost some weight but at that point people thought I would put it back on once I'd recovered from the glandular fever.

Because she now liked her new look, Wendy began restricting the foods she ate.

I started to cut down on sweets, cakes, biscuits, et cetera. But at this stage I still used to eat normal portions of everything. As the months progressed I began to get into a system of setting myself a target weight – I'd lose two or three pounds – and when I did lose weight I felt a sense of achievement. But the two or three pounds were never really enough. It never reached the point where I would stop. It was like an addiction because it gave me such a good feeling. So when I lost some weight, I just carried on doing it.

Over three years Wendy's weight dropped to five stone. Sometimes it would rise, then stick at the same level or drop again.

I would eat a lot of raw vegetables. I guess I chose them because they were bulky and filled me up. Of course, calories were also a concern.

As I mentioned earlier, anorexics are always hungry and continually thinking about food. Wendy was no exception.

Initially you are hungry but you get used to the hunger. I remember feeling light-headed and dizzy. But then I would almost get to the point where I rode over it. However painful or giddy, the self-control and the powerful anorexic side was always stronger.

Wendy doesn't believe there was one single trigger factor for the development of her anorexia.

When I was younger I used to do a lot of ballet dancing. I had to stop when I was about fourteen because of an injury to my ankle. It was a great disappointment to me and I always pined to be a dancer. If ever I went to see a ballet I'd want to be up there on the stage.

Looking back, I was very upset at the time the anorexia began. We had family problems. My father's company went bankrupt and he later went to prison. Although, having said that, this problem of mine started before all that – it wasn't the initial trigger. I think lots of things triggered it. It must have had something to do with me still wanting to be a ballet dancer, and also I wanted control. I'm an exceedingly self-disciplined person, a workaholic and a perfectionist. I'm getting better now. I've always been a neat person, everything has had to be neat and well organized – my room, for example. And my handwriting always had to be neat.

I'm aware now that I was very self-critical. I had low self-esteem and low self-confidence. I went to an all-girls school and I remember very much feeling that I wasn't as pretty and not as popular. Now I'd say that I'm just the same as everyone else. I take care and think about my appearance but I can put it into perspective. I am the way I am and to hell with everyone else.

I'm not a grade-A student but academically I was fine. I'd never put my hand up in class to answer a question – just in case it was wrong and I would look a fool. I would kick myself when someone else answered and said what I was going to say.

The strain on Wendy's family was tremendous:

For the first couple of years I lived at home and then went on to college to study speech therapy. My family were very worried, especially when it looked as if I had lost some more weight. I think that my anorexia began in the January and I didn't see a doctor until October. My mother wanted me to go to the doctor as she felt there was something wrong straight away. She tried all summer to persuade me. I was annoyed by this because she was trying to take away that bit of control I had over things, though deep down I knew she was right. Yet I was desperately frightened of putting on weight. And if I had gone to the doctor that would have meant putting on more weight. So, of course, I became very frightened of that. It must have been hell for my parents.

Wendy did see a psychiatrist but at this stage she wasn't ready to be helped.

You sit and nod your head in agreement and say that you'll try. But you come out thinking that you'll rebel and lose even more weight just to prove to them. I don't even know what I was trying to prove. It wasn't until I *wanted* to get better that the doctors' help really worked.

Wendy's denial and rebellion carried on for a couple of years until her physical condition prevented her from taking up her career as a speech therapist.

I had done eighteen months of my course. My anorexia didn't affect my studying funnily enough, I still managed to pass. I was on a placement and my weight was at its lowest. I suddenly became very low and ill. I knew I couldn't go on doing a full day's work as a speech therapist when I was only five stone. I was afraid to walk very far in case I fainted. I was continually freezing cold and had very poor circulation. Even in summer I would pile on the layers and I felt ten times worse in the winter.

I generally felt very depressed. I went to the doctor and asked to be put in hospital. My college was fantastic and told me to take as long as I liked to get better and my place was kept open for me. I was lucky, I saw a psychiatrist and the following day I was admitted to hospital. I had been prepared for a two-month wait for a bed. I don't know whether I would be here now if I had had to wait that long.

I do wish I had sought help sooner. But if I had been put in hospital against my will I don't know if the result would have been anywhere near as good as going there on my own choice. My treatment was very good. I was in a psychiatric hospital and was the only anorexic, which was good because there was no one to compare me to. I had preferential treatment and was given my own room if I wanted to study. Having volunteered for help I suppose the staff knew I wasn't going to try to cheat. Everything was discussed openly with me and I could say if I didn't agree with something. I was allowed personal possessions, and was always allowed to see my mother. After the first week I could have other people – of course I had to show signs of improvement. I was allowed to go to the toilet on my own and was never blatantly followed or checked up on. I was never forced to eat anything. I was allowed to choose my food from the trolley. If I wanted to eat lasagne and a baked potato I could, rather than have stodgy mashed potato loaded with calories. And I could eat with everyone else.

I was in hospital for six weeks. For the last three weeks I was allowed to have weekends at home. My mother was so relieved and delighted. By the time I went into hospital I was at a stage where very soon I would have been forced to go there, so my mother had been at her wits' end. After the initial shock of going into hospital it was a huge relief for me, too, to pass the control over to someone else.

Now I feel fine about food. Since regaining the weight I've lost I've got a proper woman's body and I'm proud of that. I used to look like a Belsen victim. I was hideous. I had jagged hips. My ribs stuck out at the front and back. My arms were hideously concave. I was very like a stick insect. My face became quite gaunt. I didn't lose any hair, although my periods stopped. For a little while I began exercising – jogging and aerobics – but that soon stopped as the fatigue got to me.

Since then I've discovered that I've now got low bone density, which has to be monitored. I've fractured my finger twice in my sleep. I'm taking calcium and the bone density is beginning to rise. We were petrified when I first found out. I'd lost 25 per cent of the bone density in my back and hips, which is quite a substantial amount.

Fortunately Wendy *wanted* to be helped before it was too late and thankfully she doesn't believe the anorexia will return.

I don't feel I will lapse back. It was such a painful time and such a battle to get out of. I'm also aware of how much I hurt everyone else. It was such a high when I got better, I felt as if I was being given a new life. That alone was such a good feeling that I couldn't trade that in.

I do watch what I eat but only in a healthy way. If I want

something I will eat it. Not having eaten sweet things for three years I have gone off a lot of things. As far as going out to dinner or going on a holiday is concerned, I'll eat like everybody else. I used to think about food twenty-four hours a day. I had vivid dreams that I had eaten a doughnut and I'd wake up in a sweat, wondering whether or not I really had. I was interested in cooking, which then meant I would take more of an interest in recipes. And I enjoyed wandering around a supermarket. Nowadays going to the supermarket is a chore. It wasn't such a chore then as I would check the calorific values of everything I bought. No-go areas for me were chocolate, anything cakey, chips, anything oily, margarine, butter and things like that. I cut out meat and was pretty much a vegetarian – but not because of the poor animals, I was merely thinking of the calories.

The really bad thing about anorexia is that those on the outside – carers or doctors – cannot do anything for you unless you want to do it for yourself. I could have had all the help in the world but I would not have accepted it. I am sure that is why so many anorexics die, because they never get to the point of *wanting to be helped*. But I would say, just get help and *try*, even though the thought is terrifying. It's such a wonderful thing afterwards to feel so much better. I'm happier now and I've grown up an awful lot.

3: BULIMIA NERVOSA

WHAT IS BULIMIA?

Eating disorders are totally overwhelming, the expression of extreme psychological and emotional agitation. Bulimia nervosa is no exception – it's a disorder that completely controls the sufferer's every waking moment. I've lost count of the number of sufferers who have told me that unless you have suffered from it, it's very difficult to understand just how a victim feels.

Bulimia causes the sufferer to go on a binge, when they eat huge quantities of food and just cannot stop eating. And when they're not eating they can't stop *thinking* about food. Breakfast may consist of packets of biscuits, loaves of bread, cakes, a box of doughnuts; lunch could be a whole chicken and an enormous plate of salad; with an even more enormous evening meal of pork chops and mounds of vegetables followed by a whole trifle. Then during the night a sufferer could creep downstairs and raid the fridge or cupboards and eat anything she can find. However, to avoid weight gain, the sufferer will vomit back all the food, or take large quantities of laxatives or diuretics to 'purge' the body of what they have just eaten.

Bulimia is an obsession in which almost every minute of every hour is consumed with thinking about shopping for food, cooking, bingeing and preventing weight gain. Sufferers describe themselves as prisoners – their prison walls the confines of the kitchen and bathroom. They hate what they do. They hate themselves for doing it. And they hate the fact that they cannot stop. All these feelings just add to their belief that they are failures.

Food can be a source of comfort for everyone at some time or another. But for bulimics that need for comfort begins to control their life. They eat, yet are terrified of becoming fat. They cannot resist the temptation to binge but are consumed with guilt over what they've done. The guilt fuels them on in the vicious circle to get rid of all the food they've eaten. Everything is done to extremes, yet sufferers are ensnared in a trap which reinforces their already highly developed feelings of guilt, shame, disgust and self-hatred. They feel they cannot trust themselves not to repeat their behaviour over and over again. So they binge on food in secret, then starve themselves, endure self-induced vomiting, or takes laxatives and diuretics. They believe that the whole unpleasant procedure of ridding themselves of food punishes them for not having the willpower to avoid over-eating in the first place, or they see it as a penance for the sin of bingeing, or simply as a way to avoid putting on the weight they are so terrified of.

After a day of bingeing, some sufferers will try to diet and hardly eat a thing until the irresistible urge to binge starts all over again.

When bulimia is at its worst, episodes of bingeing and vomiting can occur several times a day – very often when a sufferer is bored, worried, lonely, sad, angry, frustrated, after a bad day at the office, or an argument with a partner – the triggers for a binge are numerous and vary from sufferer to sufferer.

Premenstrual tension (these days referred to as premenstrual syndrome) is even thought to trigger a binge as it is due to a hormonal imbalance which takes place each month as the body adjusts itself in readiness for menstruation. These changes can reduce blood sugar levels. If a sufferer is rather sensitive to these changes she may want to eat more sweet things than normal in the run-up to her period.

Our body's automatic way of controlling the level of sugar circulating in the blood may be in part responsible for the need to binge. Some people more than others seem to respond to their own circulating adrenalin – the hormone responsible for releasing our sugar stores. It is released between meals so that our blood-sugar levels remain constant and can therefore keep the tissues of our bodies well supplied with energy-giving sugars.

But adrenalin is also the 'anxiety' hormone, which is released very quickly when we are frightened to prepare us for either 'flight or fight'. It causes unpleasant feelings, from butterflies in the stomach to absolute panic, with tension and irritability thrown in. Consequently, bulimic sufferers may be particularly sensitive to adrenalin and feel the need to eat to relieve the unwelcome symptoms.

And of course eating sweet food, in particular, promotes a feeling of well-being, which is why many of us weigh more than is ideal. (The feeling of well-being is caused by the surge of glucose entering the bloodstream, because the sweet substance – usually simple sugar – is much more quickly digested than other nutrients such as protein or fat.) The bulimic sufferer is likely to be eating to excess at any time of discomfort, so it is not surprising that pre-menstrual symptoms such as headaches, bloatedness and general feelings of irritability trigger a binge.

WHO IS LIKELY TO DEVELOP BULIMIA?

It's hard to answer this question accurately but sufferers of bulimia tend to be slightly older than those who develop anorexia: frequently women in their early to mid-twenties who have often been overweight as children. Some specialists, however, believe it usually begins in the late teens.

It's considered to be far more common than anorexia and there could be half a million cases in Britain alone. It's thought that about three out of every hundred women will suffer from bulimia at some point in their life. The condition can even go undetected for years because sufferers generally tend to present a public image of self-confidence, happiness and success – just think of the Princess of Wales, who is said to have been a sufferer for nine years. It's difficult to be secretive about anorexia and compulsive eating because, even if sufferers are able to hide it initially, eventually their appearance will betray their secret. Not so for the bulimic, who can hide her wretchedness for as long as she can hide her vomiting or laxative-taking.

Yet behind the façade sufferers are usually deeply depressed, full of anguish, and have an appallingly low opinion of themselves. Unlike sufferers of anorexia nervosa, bulimics often appear normal: for example, they won't have quite the same emaciated appearance accompanied by the physical symptoms of a growth of fine downy hair on the body. Weight, for instance, is unlikely to be a cause of concern as it's unusual for it to be below the average for that height and frame.

The causes of bulimia are similar to anorexia: social pressure to be thin, wanting control over one part of their life, being frightened of growing up, difficult family relationships, feelings of inadequacy, depression, stress or emotional traumas. Having control over their life plays a strong part in both disorders, and sometimes the disorders do overlap – it's not unusual for a bulimic to have also suffered from anorexia for he or she may consider bulimia to be a 'way out' since it allows them to eat – which everyone is urging them to do – but without the extra food consumption affecting their weight. And an anorexic may now and then resort to self-induced vomiting or the taking of large quantities of laxatives as a way of getting rid of unwanted calories.

Bulimia nervosa is almost certainly more common within the female population, although figures range from about five in a hundred cases being male to suggesting the number could be just one in fifty cases. Some specialists believe that the equivalent disorder in men could be alcohol abuse.

Like so many behavioural conditions, I believe sufferers tend to be very sensitive people, who cannot believe that they are coping adequately with their lives even if it appears so to the general world. To most of the people they come into contact with the sufferer seems to be a perfectionist, almost to the point of obsession. But the sufferer herself has a very low opinion of herself and needs to achieve in order to prove that she is worth something.

I'm sure some sufferers will have grown up with sisters or even mothers who have been constantly dieting, and so from an early age a link is formed in their mind between slimness and happiness, achievement even. Many sufferers have told me they believe people have to be slim to be successful in life. To them good fortune doesn't smile on the overweight.

Bulimia and bingeing have become very 'fashionable' topics for discussion in the media recently, causing alarm for many women. Time and again I'm asked to explain the condition to readers or listeners who are concerned when they occasionally 'binge' on, for example, chocolate or cakes. Patches of over-eating occur in sufferers of anorexia nervosa, in people who don't have an eating disorder, or in people suffering from obesity. But in the case of bulimia a binge is eating that is *entirely out of control*. We're talking here of vast quantities of high-calorie food often being eaten in a frenzy – food that could be raw or even still frozen – sweets, chocolate, biscuits, bread, pastry, butter and cheese, in fact any combination of food.

The sad thing is that bulimics probably despise this cycle of bingeing and purging more than anyone else can imagine. Yet the desire to binge is compulsive. Their torment is far more deep-rooted than just feeling a little bit guilty because while watching a good film on television you've eaten a whole box of chocolates.

WARNING SIGNS AND PHYSICAL SYMPTOMS

What are the warning signs to look for regarding bulimia? Well, the condition of the person's teeth is one give-away – the action of frequent vomiting wears away tooth enamel, particularly on the back of the front teeth, leading to decay. They may also have spots around the mouth and a puffy face is another sign, due to swollen salivary glands, probably as a result of the acid inflammation from the regular presence of stomach acid. There may even be loss of hair, though no one knows quite why.

Sufferers are likely to feel very depressed and apathetic after a binge, and vomiting and purging can cause great discomfort in the abdomen and stomach muscles, as can eating vast quantities of food in one session.

You may notice your relative or friend is resorting to the use of diuretics or laxatives, or his or her weight seems to fluctuate. Taking laxatives or diuretics can produce side-effects of their own – not least upon the bowel muscles which can eventually lead to chronic constipation. Different laxatives work by causing different effects. Some can go to work on the large intestine, either by speeding up the progress of faecal matter through the bowel or by increasing its bulk. Stimulant laxatives, such as senna, make the bowel muscle contract to hurry the faeces along and bulk-forming laxatives, such as ispaghula, soak up water in the bowel to increase volume and make stools softer and easier to pass. When senna and other laxatives are taken in large amounts, the digesting food is hurried through the body before too much of it can be absorbed.

So constantly using laxatives can mean the medicines interfere with the normal digestive processes and essential nutrients in the diet pass straight through instead of being absorbed into the body. The risk of vitamin and mineral deficiencies alone is therefore one good reason not to adopt this practice.

Diuretics act on the kidneys to promote urine secretion – that is, an extra output of salt and water from the body. They do this by stopping the normal retention of salt by the kidneys, allowing the excess liquid to be 'drawn' away by the salt into the urine. Potassium levels can be lowered as a result of taking some diuretics, leading to weakness and confusion.

Medication is sometimes abused by bulimics in order to achieve weight loss. An article in the *British Medical Journal* reported that there have been incidences of bulimics taking excess amounts of paracetamol in order to induce vomiting after an unusually large binge. Paracetamol abuse of this nature is referred to as Persistent Titrated Self-Poisoning. It's an extremely dangerous practice as large doses can cause serious damage to the liver and kidneys. People who have taken an overdose of paracetamol may even appear well for the following three days but can then succumb to liver damage. And those who are chronically malnourished, for example someone who has anorexia and bulimia, will be even more sensitive to the toxic effects of the drug. The dangers of using paracetamol in this way cannot be emphasized too strongly. This otherwise good and useful painkiller can become a lethal weapon when misused.

Constant diarrhoea or vomiting can cause the body to become dehydrated with the risk that essential minerals are lost. Mineral depletion can make you feel weak and faint. In more serious cases it can lead to exhaustion, stupor, coma and even death.

In a healthy person, water is essential in order to maintain normal body functions. Its importance is underlined by the fact that around half our body weight is water. Normally our kidneys balance the water lost in the urine and through perspiration against our fluid intake. For example, we pass less urine in hot weather because we can perspire several litres in a day. Consequently, our kidneys concentrate the waste that we need to pass and conserve the body's water content for the temporarily more important job of keeping our temperature stable. Also, our thirst is stimulated so that we drink more in hot weather.

Other side-effects of bulimia can be a chronic sore throat – hardly surprising when you consider how repeated vomiting can irritate the tissues of the throat. The monthly cycle can be interrupted and periods can become erratic. Dehydration can also mean poor skin.

Like anorexia, bulimia also has serious long-term implications. Osteoporosis may result (see page 21), and, as I've already mentioned, mineral depletion can occur. A sufferer may experience mouth ulcers; stomach and bowel problems; hair loss, gum disease; mouth and throat irritations.

Bulimia, like other eating disorders, can also destroy relationships. These days some couples are even citing bulimia as a reason for divorce. A report in the *Guardian* stated that one leading matrimonial lawyer has handled three cases in a year in which the wife's bulimia was cited as a fundamental reason for the break-up. The report also pointed out how a husband's bulimia was cited in a divorce petition.

Bulimia can ruin all aspects of life, both personal and professional. A normal social life and career can be difficult to maintain because of the time it takes to binge and then purge, and the exhaustion that inevitably follows.

DIFFERENCES BETWEEN BULIMIA AND ANOREXIA

Some of my listeners and readers seem confused about the differences between anorexia and bulimia because although they are usually talked about as separate conditions, patients can suffer from the symptoms of both.

One learned professor has recently opined that anorexics seem to be reacting to an internal – albeit a psychological – problem, but bulimics seem much more vulnerable to the emotional climate in which they live. It's possible that the new pressures on women and the lack of certainty about their role may be causing a change in the pattern of eating disorders. These particularly vulnerable women would be more likely to react in an extreme way to extra stress.

Another difference between anorexia and bulimia is, as I explained earlier, that an anorexic will visibly lose weight while a bulimic can look a normal size and appear to be outgoing and successful, though in reality she has little or no self-confidence.

And the bulimic pattern actually sets in quite quickly. From the odd binge in response to an upset or stress, a person will start regular bouts of over-eating. Bulimia takes hold when the sufferer discovers the ability to make herself sick. She is reassured, falsely, that she can eat as much as she wants without piling on the pounds and so gets caught up in the vicious circle of bingeing and vomiting, and drinking huge amounts of water to feel she's washing herself out.

The problem is that, to start with, bingeing is quite pleasurable, unlike anorexia where I can't imagine starving yourself can really give any pleasure. The feeling before a binge is one of great excitement and anticipation. The bulimic has a huge stash of 'naughty' foods – chocolate, ice cream, cake, biscuits. The doors may be locked and the curtains may be drawn. Some doctors even link this binge-eating with frustrated sexuality – the food a substitute for sex – though most sufferers deny this.

Apart from the obvious risks to the sufferer's health, bulimia is also expensive. Binge-eating is like a drug habit – especially if the binges are frequent – with between 10 and 15 per cent of bulimics stealing food or money to satisfy their craving. And, like a drug addiction, it is very difficult to beat without help.

TREATMENT

GPs, psychotherapists and trained counsellors have come up with ways of helping a bulimic deal with and even solve her problems, provided that she takes the first step towards seeking help. Hospitalization is a last resort, unless the person is suffering from severe depression.

As with anorexia, your first contact should be with your GP who may then refer you to a psychiatrist or psychologist who has experience in dealing with bulimia. It's useful to ask for an extended appointment with him or her so that you will have the time to discuss your problem fully. Psychotherapy may also be suggested (see page 25). This form of treatment will help you work out what might have caused the emotional turmoil that possibly triggered your chaotic pattern of eating.

Low self-esteem can be a problem when treating bulimia because so many sufferers just don't believe they're worth helping. Learning how to deal with stress and also learning how to become assertive is an important part of treating the condition. Assertiveness is about gaining control, being able to make decisions while at the same time doing what you want without stamping all over other people. When self-confidence is low people tend to be less assertive and forget that what *they* want out of life is important too.

The main aim of any treatment is usually to achieve some kind of regular eating pattern based on three meals a day, as well as the weaning off from bingeing and purging. You need to realize that you do need food to live and that to eat little and often is perfectly OK, as is eating a wide variety of food. You need to accept that being close as possible to your ideal weight is healthy for you. Trying to eat at the same time every day can help you regulate your eating habits.

The Eating Disorders Association is quite expert at advising bulimia sufferers on survival strategies. One excellent piece of advice is to use delaying tactics when you feel the urge to binge. By delaying tactics I mean go for a walk or give someone a ring – do *something* to divert your attention. (This advice can also apply to compulsive eaters or people who are overweight and want a snack.)

Don't shy away from eating with friends or family. Eating in a social situation can mean that while you are involved in conversation you forget to worry about what you are eating, or how much or how many calories there are on your plate. It also helps to eat slowly and to take smaller mouthfuls. Try to eat at regular times, and even if you have had a binge mid-morning, for example, do have lunch.

When you are out shopping buy small amounts rather than large quantities, so that when you get home you can't binge because you haven't bought bingeable quantities. In return, and if you can afford it, give yourself other harmless treats – a one-off expensive hair-do, a new item of clothing or something similar – as a thank you to yourself for starting to take control of the problem.

CASE STUDIES: HELEN AND FIONA

As I've said, many sufferers of eating disorders will have had an unhappy childhood, when the seeds of uncertainty and self-doubt were first sown. And many bulimics may also have initially had anorexia. Helen's story is such an example. Her childhood was marred by feelings of inadequacy, self-loathing and, I suggest, terrible loneliness. She never felt she had the right to express her true feelings to those around her and sadly had no one she felt she could confide in. Her weight has gone from fourteen stone to five stone and now, at twenty-eight, she is still battling with bulimia.

> When I had anorexia I would just eat an apple or a Bourbon biscuit and consider that was food so I'd vomit to bring it all back up. I was out of control.
>
> Anorexia and bulimia have taken their toll on my body. I have backache and when I had an X-ray I was told that it was a result of wear and tear – I keep bending over to be sick. I've had lots of trouble with my potassium levels. If I don't have enough potassium I am at risk of a coronary. I have to take six potassium tablets a day.
>
> All my front teeth are crowned because of the damage

the stomach acid has caused. I had to have specialist treatment at a dental hospital which took two years and was very painful and distressing. I'd cry at the slightest thing. I couldn't stand any pain, my teeth were so sensitive, but I knew it had to be done.

While Helen found the dental treatment to be exceedingly painful, she wasn't resentful that her bulimia had meant she had to have this treatment. She felt that she wasn't of any value as a person and deserved such pain.

During a lot of that time I felt I needed to be punished anyway. So I took the dental treatment as a form of punishment which I thought I deserved.

Even now Helen has a terribly low opinion of herself – although she has been able to pinpoint the root of these feelings.

When I was eleven I was sexually abused by a neighbour's friend's husband – it only happened the once, thank goodness.
I came from a family of five. I was the middle child and I felt as if I was sitting on the fence looking in. I wasn't involved in any conversation and my point of view was never taken. I felt that way from about the age of seven when my brother was born.

Helen recognized that from this time onwards she slowly but surely began a pattern of self-abuse, and not just through food. She turned her hurt back on to herself and demonstrated this by causing herself pain.

I used to sit upstairs at home and pull out my milk teeth or give myself Chinese burns. I wanted to hurt myself because I wasn't wanted. All the attention was focused on my brother.
I felt my older brother was wanted because he was the first born. My sister was wanted because she was the first

girl. Then there was me who served no purpose. My younger sister had pneumonia as a baby and nearly died so she was always made a fuss off. Then there was my little brother who was the baby of the family and spoiled rotten.

When I was younger I would eat for comfort – chips, chocolate, sweets – when I had money. At school I always felt an outsider. At thirteen or fourteen I would sit and cry and I didn't even know what I was crying for. My dad was so strict I would be frightened to go home. He used to belt us with a leather belt. He would beat me up too. He'd say I was a lazy bitch and didn't help my mother enough. He would come home with friends and have a drink and then he would show off in front of them about what a macho man he was. So I grew up thinking I must deserve what I got.

I started to diet when I was seventeen. At first I was sensible. I was already a compulsive eater – I would think nothing of eating fish and chips three times a day and things like that. I began by cutting out potatoes and bread. I lost weight and was ten stone but my weight seemed to stick at that level for ages. I'm five foot three. I wanted to be thin because I felt that fat people didn't get on in society and that if I changed my shape and size I would be accepted.

When I was fat, people would call me names and think that I didn't have any feelings. I had no one to turn to or just talk to and I was bullied at school. I started to stick my fingers down my throat and began taking laxatives. I think I read about people doing that and thought it was a good way of losing weight.

Fortunately for Helen there was one person who was noticeably concerned and who acted to help her.

I went to a youth club and there the youth leader began to be concerned about me and the weight I was losing. She encouraged me to go to what was then called Anorexic Aid. I never thought that I looked any different – I thought I was fat even when I had lost nine stone. I saw a psychologist at a drop-in clinic who told me I needed to see a doctor. I saw the doctor for about a year. She put me on anti-depressants and weighed me every week. She told me that if I got a job I would get out of my depression. I hated myself. I still loathe myself. I didn't want to get a job, I just wanted to die. I told her I hated her too and was referred to a psychiatrist.

Helen was reluctant to be admitted to a psychiatric hospital because of the stigma attached, even though she was now becoming desperately ill and was in danger of falling into a coma at any time. In hospital she had complete bed rest, as well as treatment for her depression and ECT (electroconvulsive therapy). Like many anorexia sufferers, she thoroughly resented the way she was treated in hospital.

I wasn't allowed to have a bath. They washed me. I wasn't allowed to exercise, or get dressed, not allowed to listen to music on my personal stereo. When I went to the toilet I was escorted – they didn't want me to burn off any calories. They gave me hot milk with added vitamins and I had to eat normal food – chicken, mashed potato, et cetera – food I wouldn't normally eat. Some days I ate it and other days I threw it away. I felt as though my rights had been completely taken away from me.

Then I realized that the only way I would get out of hospital would be to put on weight and reach a target of seven and a half stone. So I decided I would eat just to get out of hospital. I was twenty at the time. I'm twenty-eight now. When I came out of hospital I was supposed to see a social worker but she never turned up. All my life I feel as if I've kept slipping through the net.

I sincerely believe that Helen's experience in hospital and subsequently is not at all typical and that most patients receive the care and attention they deserve. And, despite all Helen's unhappiness, she still firmly recommends that 'sufferers get help before it's too late'.

Helen is also an example of a young woman who continually seems to escape the love, attention and compassion that she needs the most.

I had one happy time when I worked with brain-damaged children. I stayed with a family who had a ten-year-old boy who was brain-damaged. I would still eat obsessively and that was when my anorexia turned to bulimia. I'd eat crisps, sandwiches, fruit, Coke, chocolate, in large amounts. I would never tell anyone.

When I then went to live back home the family made fun of me. After a meal they'd say: there she goes, she's off to be sick. My older brother even used to call me names. He'd call me Anna, short for anorexia. I always used to be taunted.

Recently Helen has been trying to cope with her life and its problems.

For the last three years I've been going to a centre for people with mental health problems. I go five days a week. We do all sorts of things to boost our confidence and to get us out into the community. I still take anti-depressants, tranquillizers and sleeping tablets – I can't imagine that I will ever be off tablets. I've tried to kill myself five times – I hate myself.

I get annoyed with myself now and again because I really do want to be better – but I want to run before I can walk. I can't help myself, which is why I have set up a self-help group.

We don't offer any miracles but I would advise anyone who wants to diet to get help from a proper dietician. I feel if I had been taken seriously when I wanted to lose weight I might not be in the situation I am now. I don't think I was taken seriously because I was a child who wanted to lose weight. I still suffer from bulimia but it is more under control. I keep my breakfast down, which is two slices of toast – that's all I have. If I eat any more I have to be sick. I feel so guilty. I'm ten stone five pounds now and if I'm honest I would like to be thin again. I just feel I can cope when I don't eat – yet there's not a minute goes by without me thinking about food. And I still believe that you have to be thin to get on in life. I feel bulimia is feeding my depression.

Support is so vital, I feel that if I had had counselling ten years ago I would be better now. People with eating disorders need to be listened to and given time to grow into their own personalities. My advice to other sufferers would be go and get help before it's too late. Bulimia is a compulsion that rules your life.

Whereas Helen is still struggling to beat bulimia, Fiona, a thirty-five-year-old environmental health technician who suffered from bulimia for just over sixteen years, has been clear of the condition for more than five years.

To start with I didn't realize I had bulimia. I was mixed up at that time and it wasn't until I was fifteen or sixteen that I realized I had an eating disorder. I didn't know where to go for help.

I was about thirteen and overweight. I wanted to lose about a stone and a half. I didn't feel comfortable the way I was. It was quite difficult to get clothes to fit me. It was embarrassing. I didn't wear trousers that much. If I wanted anything to fit it was then always too long. I felt heavy.

I must have read about someone eating and making themselves sick in a magazine or a newspaper. I lost about two stone over a period of about six months. To me making myself sick seemed like a good idea because it kept my parents happy – I was losing weight while at the same time they could see me eating. But I didn't feel comfortable about it really. I was in conflict.

I didn't eat anything at school. At home I had to eat or my parents would notice. At first I was sick once or twice a day. I don't think I found it unpleasant I just got on with it. Sometimes I would feel a bit ashamed afterwards because I associated being sick with being ill, so I thought I was making myself ill, and it was a bit sneaky as well.

Like so many bulimia sufferers Fiona kept her secret to herself – until the age of twenty-eight, when she decided she had to get help once and for all.

I never told anyone. Bulimia kept my weight at the same level and stopped me putting on weight. I did feel happier when I was thinner. I used to get teased a lot at school and out playing on the estate where I lived. They called me Fiona Fatgut. They said I wobbled rather than walked. I was overweight. I'd developed breasts, for example, and I hadn't bought a bra so I suppose I did wobble.

I had been brought up in a small farming community. My parents had been evicted from the house and so we'd moved to the estate. My parents argued a lot at this time and I was more sensitive than my sister. On the estate I was taken aback by the other children, who were more street-wise. I had never been the centre of attention before. I went to a mixed school and was top of the class. Boys used to get their own back for that by taunting me. I felt very much alone. But I would always say I was OK and put on a brave face. I always seemed happy-go-lucky.

As Fiona got older the problem became worse, particularly at the time of her A levels and when she left home to go to university.

Also at seventeen or eighteen I was more aware of boys and I suppose I wanted to look good. By now I could be sick three or four times a day of a weekend. My parents went out working, and so did my sister, so I was often on my own at home. I was relieved to find myself alone, as I didn't have to be so secretive about vomiting.

When I left home at eighteen and went to university it got worse. Now there was no restraint. If I wanted to make myself sick I could. Then I would make myself sick whenever I ate. It was habit. If I ate, I would be sick.

With bulimia you don't look at food as a source of nourishment. I looked at food in terms of what was OK to eat and what was not OK to eat. Salad or meat and two veg was fine, but sweets and snack stuff didn't feel right. If I was in company I would eat the food and switch off, but if I was on my own it would bother me. In company I would leave early or I would miss lectures simply to make myself sick.

When I lodged with friends they tried to talk to me about it. They would say they had heard someone being sick. They didn't say, 'Fiona, you make yourself sick.' I kept denying it by saying they must have heard the next-door neighbour. I was ashamed to admit it was me because people would have looked at me strangely, as if I was mad. Then they would probably just say, 'Why?'

After I left university I got married and lived in Germany. My then husband was in the Army. He was away a lot and I was away from my family. I felt even more isolated. I found socializing difficult – people were interested in other things. Most had children which I didn't. So I was on my own a lot and sometimes I'd make myself sick in the morning and just carry on through the day. I'd buy crisps, cakes, ice cream, anything. I'd buy chocolate knowing that I was buying it to eat to make myself sick. Your mind is programmed that way.

I'd eat, then be sick, then I might have to go to bed for a while because being sick so much is quite tiring. I had no control. I would eat large quantities of food – a whole family packet of crisps, half a loaf was nothing to me, anything that was there, tins, I'd defrost food from the freezer. Even now it's difficult to imagine that I could eat that amount of food.

While I was eating it was quite pleasant. But I constantly had a bad stomach from being so full. I'd also get stomach cramps and feel as if I had an ulcer. I had a constant sore throat. I have loads of fillings in my back teeth.

I never did tell my husband, from whom I'm now divorced. The marriage had lots of problems and I suppose the bulimia didn't help. But sometimes I feel it kept me sane. My husband was manipulative and violent towards me at times. Food was my comfort in a very unhappy marriage. Several times I wanted to leave and finally, after seven years, I couldn't take any more.

Fiona eventually went to a support group for people with eating disorders.

At the group it was suggested I go to my GP. He was tremendous and referred me to a clinical psychologist. By this time I'd bought books on the subject and tried to read as much as I could about it. The psychologist helped me to express myself better – that if I didn't want to do something I could say no, which I never did at work. I didn't want other people to think that I was a bad person.

There's no way you can stop eating, as food is so readily available. I see it as an addiction. You think about food all the time. And if a person hasn't learnt how to deal with their emotions it's difficult to sustain recovery. You have to want to get better because it's hard work. Sometimes bulimia was a stress-reliever for me. If I got worked up I'd eat and be sick. I don't know which of the two was the stress-reliever. I had to learn that I just had to sit down after eating and not move for fifteen minutes. That's something you have to work through yourself. There's so much inner turmoil involved you have to want to do it for yourself. Now I note down what's upsetting me or work out what a problem is by writing things out.

I do believe I have recovered but I'm aware that if I found myself in a certain situation I would have a tendency to go back. It took me three years in all to get out of the habit of eating and making myself sick. Whether or not that feeling is my own safety valve, I don't know.

4: COMPULSIVE EATING

WHAT IS COMPULSIVE EATING?

When people are unhappy or stressed many turn to alcohol or light up a cigarette. Some people resort to drug abuse. Others binge on comfort food – many compulsive eaters say that when anything goes wrong they head straight for the fridge.

None of the above are healthy ways of facing up to problems, all are 'ways out' that just bring more problems in the end. And I've never heard anyone who gorges themselves on more food than they can comfortably eat say they feel good about themselves, their body image or the way they eat. That alone is a very stressful way to live.

Compulsive eating means eating when you're not at all hungry without having the willpower to stop. It can be described as a way of managing anxiety through the (usually secret) use of food. Sufferers feel they have no control over their lives. They feel totally dissatisfied with themselves and are ashamed of their lack of self-discipline. They may feel isolated, lonely and unhappy, whether through family problems or a traumatic event, such as bereavement or divorce.

Just like anorexia and bulimia sufferers, they become obsessed with food. They have a complete preoccupation with body image, and a dreaded fear of being fat. In fact, compulsive eating could be thought of as a kind of bulimia, the difference being that a compulsive eater will eat and eat and eat, without worrying about getting rid of the food she has consumed. She doesn't vomit or use laxatives or go on an excessive exercise drive, but she's still eating as a way of dealing with an underlying problem. She will eat for comfort rather than face up to what is making her behave this way.

When you can't face up to problems and express the way you are feeling in words, you're eventually likely to express your emotions in some other way. Experts consider that some people eat compulsively as a result of this. They try to stuff their emotions down their throats, in a desperate bid to keep their feelings subjugated. Others say that over-eating is a means of defiance, in other words defying social pressures to be 'normal'.

So who is likely to become a compulsive eater? One interesting fact is that men seem to suffer from compulsive eating far more than any other eating disorder. And also, apparently, there is quite a high incidence of compulsive eating in the caring professions, where carers tend to put everyone else first and their own needs second. The irregular hours and the heavy responsibility for others' lives makes them seek solace in food.

What makes someone a *compulsive eater* rather than someone who just likes food? Well, a compulsive eater will be a person who probably *hates* food – because of the way it affects her life. A compulsive eater could be someone who does not appear to eat too much – a woman, say, who doesn't eat breakfast because she is too busy getting the children off to school. Yet when the children are out of the house she will eat everything that is left on the table. Then she'll nibble on a packet of biscuits and go on nibbling throughout the day, rather than sitting down to healthy meals.

One thing's for sure, food will provide her with comfort, an emotional crutch to which she becomes addicted. Just as the alcoholic becomes addicted to drink, the compulsive eater is addicted to food, even though she hates what it's doing to her. The alcoholic may seek solace at the bottom of a beer glass when he rarely finds it in reality; the compulsive eater will seek solace in a supermarket, buying all sorts of different food. Her self-loathing once she's eaten everything is just the same as the alcoholic's.

She may also be hooked on dieting and have tried every diet in every magazine, from high-fibre to high-protein. Each time, she puts all the weight back on once the dieting has ceased.

Just as anorexia and bulimia lead to long-term health risks, so does compulsive eating. Not surprisingly it can lead to obesity, with all its associated health risks (see page 65), depression, mood changes and irritability, problems with metabolism and, in some rare cases, even a ruptured stomach.

TREATMENT

Compulsive eaters may be helped by making sure they eat at the same time every day. All they need to do is follow a sensible eating plan, not a crash diet.

If you are a compulsive eater and are overweight, you should seek the help of your GP. Other options include counselling, because you will need to look at your life and why you have developed these frenzied eating habits. The causes can be the same as those for bulimia, and the treatment for these two conditions are also very similar.

CASE STUDY: ANNIE

Annie, now a thirty-four-year-old teacher, was a compulsive eater for the three years she spent at teacher training college. With hindsight she understands why she behaved in this way – although at the time she didn't know what was happening, just that eating made her feel secure in a strange, new world after leaving home.

Going to college was something I'd looked forward to for ages. I hadn't thought that I might feel insecure about leaving home. After all, at eighteen you think you're grown up, know it all and you just long to be independent. I hadn't prepared myself for the fact that sitting alone in my room in a hall of residence I might begin to feel so lonely. I hadn't even thought that this might be perfectly natural because I come from quite a close family with lots of relatives living nearby – there was always someone popping into our house. I only realized this years afterwards. At the time I just thought I wasn't being grown up enough. I didn't tell anyone about how lonely I would feel at night and at the weekends – I didn't feel lonely while I was at college during the day. And that was when I started to eat.

At first, I would eat what I considered to be healthy things that wouldn't make me put on weight. But the things I loved were bananas and avocados – probably about the most fattening of fruit and vegetables. I started to eat a couple at a time but gradually I would eat six bananas in one go, then avocados, then round after round of toast. Some people chain smoke, but when I felt really low and lonely I would chain eat. Then I'd hate myself the next morning when my jeans began to feel too tight. I'd hate my body too.

During that first year at college Annie put on two stone in weight. She's just over five feet and soon weighed eleven stone. But it was during her second and third years that her weight increased even further and she put on three more stone.

I really ballooned in size and soon gave up my jeans. I began to make my own clothes. It was easier to sew my own things – that way I didn't have to admit to anyone just how fat I was or what size I was. When I went shopping with my flatmates they would be buying clothes to fit size 10 or 12.

I don't think the shops we went into would have had anything to fit me anyway. But I never admitted that to my friends. I just used to ramble on and on about what a rip-off boutiques were and how I hated to have the same clothes as everyone else. It was much easier to talk myself into believing that than admit that I was desperately unhappy and longed to wear the same fashionable things they did instead of slumming it in my big baggy pinafore dresses which hid every lump and bump.

Annie can recognize that at this time she had little self-confidence and terribly low self-esteem. She had little contact with members of the opposite sex and was very shy. Her friends didn't seem to be at all shy and this only served to make her feel worse. To compensate for her lack of self-confidence she would eat.

I remember walking into the refectory at lunchtime. By this time I would have already eaten the packed lunch I'd made earlier in the day. I would intend to have just a cup of tea. But here again everybody would be sitting at tables seemingly laughing and joking effortlessly with boys. I'd join my course friends at the table and I would feel so shy and intimidated that I wouldn't know what to do with myself. So, in order to give me something to do and make me feel comfortable, I would get myself a plate of chips. By sitting at the table eating I didn't feel that I had to join in the conversation, even though I longed to.

My friends would inevitably say something along the lines of 'There she goes, eating again.' I used to hate them for saying it and hate myself for wanting to eat more food. It felt as if they were pointing a finger at me or pointing me out to everyone else so that everyone on the table could have a laugh at the fat person's expense yet again.

Going out for the evening, say, to a party on a Saturday night, would be awful too. Before we started to get ready, have showers and get dressed up, the girls would all talk about who they fancied. I never used to join in these conversations because I knew there was no point, nobody would fancy me anyway. While they used to get excited at the prospect of being chatted up, I dreaded going. I knew I'd be the wallflower again. I'd just stick near the party food – if there was any – to give myself something to do.

Mealtimes back at her flat were terrible for Annie. Again her lack of self-confidence made her reject the food her friends ate. She'd come from a working-class background and thought her new friends considered her socially inferior. These feelings added to her sense of inadequacy.

They were always cooking things with lots of garlic. I couldn't bear to tell them that I had never even tasted garlic before. I just used to reject what they cooked, claiming to prefer plain food. I used to keep my own food in the end. I had a cardboard box in the corner of the kitchen in which I had packets of custard cream biscuits underneath the vegetables. I'd get up in the middle of the night and sometimes eat four packets in a row, in secret.

Looking back I realize that the way I felt was my own fault. I'm sure my flatmates didn't deliberately try to poke fun at me, or ridicule me. If they didn't like me or value my company they would never have wanted to share a flat with me. Of course, I've lost touch with them now, and sometimes I feel quite sad because at last I have the self-esteem and confidence to be able to talk about those times – because there were some good times in between all the eating!

When I left college I went back home to live. There I didn't feel so lonely, just loved for being me. My family didn't tease me or comment on how much I was eating or whether I was 'eating again'.

I got a job as a primary teacher at a local school. There, too, the children began to like me as their teacher. I felt good about myself for the first time in a long while. I felt the children accepted me for what I was. They just saw me as their teacher, not the fat girl. In time I found that I didn't need to comfort my own feelings of inadequacy by eating lots of food. For the first time in my life I felt as if I had confidence and for the first time I began to like myself. Slowly I began to lose weight, which I have to admit did make me feel better about myself. I'm now a size 14. I'll never be the type of person who is really slim but that doesn't bother me. I'm happy the way I am.

5: OBESITY

We are all becoming more and more health-conscious thanks to campaigns about heart disease, exercise and so on, but whether we are all taking notice of this new-found awareness remains to be seen. Obesity, for instance – carrying more fat than your body needs – is thought to be a huge problem in the Western world. Some experts believe that about a third of adults in this country are so overweight that it is posing a threat to their health and life-expectancy.

Government figures have recently confirmed this worry after a special campaign, aimed to reduce the number of obese men by a quarter and the number of obese women by a third, has statistics which clearly show that as a nation we are becoming fatter. The numbers are *up* not down. The latest reports show that in 1991 13 per cent of men and 15 per cent of women are overweight, compared with 7 per cent and 12 per cent in 1986. The Health Secretary, Virginia Bottomley, has blamed modern living and the high number of people who have sedentary jobs while taking little exercise.

It also looks as though we still eat far too much fat, although according to a survey produced by the Ministry of Agriculture, Fisheries and Food we are eating less lard, butter and hard margarines, and using un-saturated fat instead. For example, we are now eating a quarter less butter than we did in 1975.

The National Food Survey also showed that whole-meal bread now has a larger share of the market than white and that in general people ate less fat and more fruit and vegetables in 1992. Millions of people are also switching from full-fat milk to low-fat. And people apparently also eat fewer bought cakes and pastries. So despite these slightly encouraging trends, it is disappointing that we are continuing to get fatter.

Obesity is thought to be the biggest killer in the Western world, along with smoking, and even though it is quite straightforward to diagnose, treating it may not be so easy.

So when does being overweight turn into being obese? For a woman personal health risks due to obesity begin when you are 30 per cent overweight. For a man the figure is 25 per cent. For example, if your ideal weight is around ten stone, once you reach thirteen stone you are putting yourself at risk. If a man weighs 12 stone ideally, his health may suffer if he puts on three stone or more. In these instances, obesity can be seen as a disease that can shorten your life, and make you ill far more often and in a variety of ways (from heart attacks to arthritis, via chest infections). Indeed, there are few illnesses which aren't made worse by such levels of obesity. But for everyday purposes I believe that we should all be aware of the need to control our weight once we are 10 per cent or more above our ideal.

I think the best definition of being too fat is this: if you stand stark naked before a full-length mirror and bob up and down, nothing should wobble, except the saucy bits! (In technical terms that's the external genitalia for a man and the breasts for a woman!)

Obesity can be divided into three categories – cosmetic obesity (when a person is mildly overweight); medical obesity (your weight is 135 per cent what it should be); and morbid obesity. A morbidly obese person is one who is seven stone or more overweight. Some people can be 15 stone overweight. When you're morbidly obese you pose a serious threat to your life-expectancy.

WHAT CAUSES A PERSON
TO BE OVERWEIGHT?

Quite simply, if you eat more calories than your body burns up you will put on weight. It's true that your individual metabolism can play a part in how heavy you become, and it's also true that for a rare few obese people it may be due to a gland disorder. But, regrettably, far too many overweight people who do not have this disorder use it as an excuse not to do anything about their weight. Another regularly used cop-out is to say, 'I'm big boned.' The ideal weight for your height, as shown by responsible charts or the Body Mass Index (page 108), is probably the most straightforward of all guides.

Genetically, you are at risk of being overweight if your parents are or were too, and it's not just because of your genes. If your parents are overweight, it's likely that they have big appetites and you, by their example, have also developed a big appetite. Certainly in the past children were encouraged to 'eat it all up' when an enormous plate of food was put before them. The next few words of encouragement were, 'Go on – it's good for you.' But eating far more than your body needs or wants is far from good for you.

Some reports point out that around half of all middle-aged women who have a weight problem say that they put on weight and never lost it again during and after a pregnancy. It is my opinion that this is because this extra weight can be harder to shift and most of us find any extra weight difficult to remove when it doesn't melt away naturally. Exercise and dieting in combination is usually the only way to do it, requiring considerable determination for many if not most of us.

Another reason for being overweight could be that we tend to eat by the clock – if it's one o'clock it must be time for lunch – rather than eating when we are actually hungry. We also eat the types of food we have been accustomed to eat rather than food which may be of a lower fat content and therefore more healthy. Some people over-eat just because they are in the habit of it.

And it's not surprising that so many adults turn to food for comfort when they are unhappy, depressed or stressed, when you consider how foods are used in childhood. Weren't you ever given chocolates, biscuits, sweets, et cetera, for being a good girl or boy? Or were you ever told you couldn't have treats because you hadn't been good enough?

And there is more. It can now be considered politically incorrect to point out the dangers of being seriously overweight. My position is this: once the dangers have been pointed out, then adults must decide for themselves. If anyone thinks fat is beautiful I would not agree or disagree – it's their choice. Perhaps the most helpful response for someone who is heavier than average and has decided to stay that way is to say, 'This is just the way I am.'

A question I'm often asked is 'Are people born fat?' As I've said, quite often fat parents have fat children. One way to test whether a personal characteristic is hereditary or due to the environment – nature or nurture – has been to study what happens to identical twins who from birth have been forced to live apart. From such studies it seems that our genes may be, in good part, to blame, although this isn't the entire cause.

Obesity more often occurs in babies and children who are encouraged, sometimes strongly, to 'eat everything up', when the amount put on their plate is far too much for them. And, earlier still, there is an understandable tendency for a bottle-fed baby to be encouraged to finish each bottle and to be weaned earlier than necessary.

All of these traits encourage over-eating, which often continues for life. Then, once a child – or adult – is overweight, they take less exercise as it becomes more of an effort.

It's a sad fact of life that slim people do tend to look down on those who are overweight, and this can be particularly hard on children. Whether we like to admit it or not, fat people are looked upon as figures of fun. Fat children may indeed find it difficult to make friends. It's even been reported that children of normal weight prefer the company of disabled children rather than fat ones. This is because, it's alleged, disabled children cannot 'help' it whereas the fat ones can!

It puzzles many that people can eat at different rates. People ask me why some get fatter than others when they seem to eat the same quantities of food? The answer is that some people burn up the calories more quickly than others.

Another question that I'm asked from time to time is whether or not you just get fatter with age? Many people believe this to be true, but in fact it is an old wives' tale. If you are putting on weight, it simply means that you are eating too much. It could be that you put on weight as you get older because you're no longer using up the same amount of energy that you did when you were younger.

If you are slightly overweight the only real problem is having to buy bigger clothes. But often, once you are overweight, that tendency has a habit of turning into obesity. It's an easy trap to fall into, especially if you are one of the many people who turn to food whenever you're unhappy or upset.

HEALTH RISKS

High blood pressure

Hypertension, to call it by its medical name, is not a disease in itself, but having it can make you more vulnerable to strokes, heart and kidney disease. When your heart beats it causes a surge of blood which raises the blood pressure. What is an abnormal blood pressure reading? Well, the first part of the reading denotes the pressure in the main arteries and heart as they pulse or beat (systolic). The second reading is the pressure between the beats (diastolic). A low blood pressure is usually a health benefit as it indicates the heart and blood vessels are not under stress. A very rough rule is that normal systolic pressure should generally be 100 plus your age, and the diastolic pressure less than 90.

Heart disease

Heart disease is the commonest cause of early death in the UK – nearly a third of all deaths in men of working age. The chances of you developing heart disease are increased when you are obese. This is because sugar, refined carbohydrates and excess animal fat can increase the fats in the blood. There are three fats in the blood: cholesterol, which comes in two forms – the 'good' type, High Density Lipoprotein (HDL), and the 'bad' type, Low Density Lipoprotein (LDL). The HDL is a kind of transporter fat. It gathers up the LDL and enables it to be safely used by the body. If the ratio of LDL to HDL rises, the excesss of LDL gets deposited on the inside of the body's artery walls, making them more likely to burst or cause the blood flowing through them to clot. This can cause such serious conditions as stroke or coronary thrombosis.

Triglycerides are the third fat circulating in the body. High levels of this fat in the blood, while also adding to the problems cause by the LDLs, are specifically associated with inflammation of the pancreas – pancreatitis. This causes a particularly distressing abdominal pain and general malaise. It is very difficult to treat successfully in its chronic form.

A raised cholesterol level in the blood is one of the most widely recognized causes of coronary artery and other heart conditions. What's more, it's not only the heart that can be affected. The cholesterol is deposited just under the lining of the heart, its arteries and all the arteries in the body. This restricts the flow of blood and so can cause coronary thrombosis – a heart attack. It can also weaken the arteries to the extent that they burst. If this happens in the brain, it's called a stroke; if it happens in the big arteries of the heart, it's a dissecting aneurysm.

That's the bad news. On the good side, reducing the level of cholesterol to a normal blood level – especially if it's done in a way that increases the proportion of good cholesterol (HDL) – can reverse much, or all, of the damage that's been done. You can do this by slimming down to your ideal weight, reducing the amount of all fats in your diet, especially the saturated variety (usually of animal origin), and by taking more regular exercise. It's also a good idea to eat proportionately more unsaturated fats and oils, such as olive and corn oils – and also fatty fish, mackerel, herring, and similar fish for the unsaturated oil that they naturally contain.

Diabetes

There are two types of diabetes: insulin-dependent diabetes and non-insulin dependent diabetes. The first is treated by insulin injections and diet. About one in four people with diabetes have this type. It's the most severe form and usually develops under the age of thirty.

Non-insulin dependent diabetes affects the remaining three out of four diabetics. It's also known as maturity-onset diabetes and is more common among elderly people, especially if they have been overweight for twenty years or more. The complications for these sufferers are due both to the obesity and to the diabetes

– which can affect the tissues of the eye, the kidneys, the heart and blood vessels and the nervous system.

Cancer

Those cancers which are more common in obese people are of the large bowel, and in women of the breast, uterus and cervix. These associations have been discovered by the epidemiologists – scientists and doctors whose research shows what the cause might be. Obviously, only a few obese people will develop cancer and there is so far no more definite guide as to which specific aspect of obesity is particularly responsible and which obese people will therefore be liable to these cancers.

Osteoarthritis

This is the most common form of arthritis, usually affecting the over-fifties. The disease causes great pain because it damages joint surfaces, thus inhibiting the painless and proper use of the joint. It mainly affects the weight-bearing joints and those in constant use, such as knees, hips, spine and fingers. When it develops, the protective, shock-absorbing rubbery substance called cartilage, which covers the ends of the bones to protect them at the joints, becomes worn and rough and is almost 'rubbed away'. In places it splits so that the bone underneath thickens and spreads out, enlarging the joint. The disease causes such damage to the surface of the joint that it can't work properly. The bones rub against each other causing pain and stiffness, particularly after the person has been still for a while.

While osteoarthritis affects some families much more than others, an obese person will suffer from it much worse than they would if they were at the ideal weight because, as I said, it affects the weight-bearing joints.

Gout

A common and extremely painful form of arthritis, gout is an inflammatory reaction caused by uric acid crystals deposited in the joints, which trigger a reaction in the tissue. While there is often a family tendency, the condition is also associated with over-eating and excessive drinking of alcohol. Consequently those who are heavily overweight are more likely to suffer than those who are not. Bingeing either on food or alcohol will often trigger an acute attack.

Gall stones

These are supposedly twice as common in obese people. They form due to an over-concentration of bile in the gall bladder. The bile, the digestive juice particularly responsible for the digestion of fat in the small intestine, is produced in the liver. When excess food is eaten this production is increased, over-concentrating its normal supply and leading to gall stones.

As well as the medical risks to your health, and the fact that death from coronary heart disease, diabetes, digestive diseases (such as indigestion, gastritis, hiatus herniae, irritable bowel and constipation) and cerebrovascular diseases (such as strokes) are more common in the obese, other consequences of obesity are psychological and emotional, just as in the other eating disorders. Being greatly overweight can make a person feel depressed, inadequate or inferior. These feelings can make them eat more as they try to comfort themselves and so sets up a vicious circle which is very difficult to break.

TREATMENT

If you have a severe weight problem, you really should see your GP for advice. Just as for the anorexia sufferer or bulimia sufferer, the first step on the road to recovery is admitting that you have a problem and want to seek help. Only *you* can decide if you want to lose weight. And you will only succeed if you *really want to*. Losing weight is hard work. It can take three months to lose two stone or even as long as five or six months, because as you lower your intake of calories, your metabolism slows, so the rate at which you lose weight decreases too.

It's quite unfair of people to claim that weight loss can be quick and easy. It rarely is. Obesity needs long-term management. There's no point strictly adhering to a four-week diet just to put all the weight back on once you've stopped dieting. You need to change your eating habits once and for all. You need to be encouraged to adopt eating patterns that you will be able to keep up with. You need to change your psychological and emotional attitude towards food. Most of all you must avoid using it as a comforter, so try to resolve any problems in your life that may be making you over-eat.

The main way to treat obesity is through a low-energy diet – but only with the advice of your doctor or a dietician. The usual amount of calories that should be consumed when you are dieting is 1000 a day. Diets providing less than 800 calories a day are not really advantageous, unless undertaken with hospital supervision. Drugs such as appetite-suppressants are not recommended as most are 'uppers' (stimulants) and addictive. Many people who take them find that they can no longer do without them and may also need to keep increasing the dose to achieve the same effect. Often the addiction rules their lives. Surgery is also not, as a rule, recommended, and a surgeon will usually only operate when the problem is severe and everything else has been tried (see pages 74–5).

If you are overweight and want to diet, you have to realize that you need to change your habits – any weight loss should be carried out under medical supervision and you should aim to reduce your weight slowly and sensibly. Healthy living doesn't mean that you have to give up all the things you enjoy eating, but it does mean making some changes that can result in a big difference to your health. You need to choose the right foods for your body – a varied diet will provide you with the nutrients, vitamins and minerals you require.

Eat plenty of foods rich in starch and fibre. Don't eat too much fat and don't eat high-sugar foods too often. If you are going to eat ready-prepared meals or foods, make sure you check the ingredients label for the fat content. Some supermarkets now have clear labelling policies for a food that is low-fat.

You'll find that starchy foods such as potatoes (baked or boiled) are satisfying, without containing too many calories. The wholegrain varieties of starchy foods – for example, wholemeal bread, flour and pastas – are recommended because they are high in fibre. Other examples are porridge oats, brown rice, baked beans, peas, lentils and sweetcorn. Fibre, the indigestible part of cereals, fruit and vegetables, is nature's laxative and so helps to prevent constipation, gall stones and other disorders of the bowel, and possibly even bowel cancer. This type of food may also help keep blood cholesterol levels low.

So cut down on fat, as eating too much of it definitely

leads to you becoming overweight and it is linked to heart disease. There are two types of fat – saturated and unsaturated. Saturates are found in meat and meat products, dairy products, hard margarines and in cooking fat. It's also in products that contain 'hidden' fat such as cakes, biscuits, puddings and chocolate, which contains a lot more fat than many of us realize. Unsaturates include polyunsaturated fats and mono-unsaturated fats. You'll find this type in vegetable oils, the popular sunflower oil, corn and soy, rape-seed or olive oil. It is also in nuts and oily fish.

You need to reduce the amount of *saturated* fat you have in your diet because it is this type that can lead to a high level of blood cholesterol (see page 67) which increases the risk of heart disease. Most saturated fats are, for example, animal fats found around meat, in butter, full-fat cheese and cream. You can roughly tell which fats they are because they will be solid at room temperature. There are two saturated plant fats, though – palm and coconut.

Use skimmed or semi-skimmed milk rather than whole milk as well as low-fat cheese. Trim off the fat when you eat meat. Eat more fish and chicken (take the skin off the chicken either before or after it it is cooked since the skin and the tissues just below it are rich in fat). Try not to fry food. Avoid meat pies, corned beef, butter, ordinary soft margarine as opposed to a low-fat spread, crisps, chocolate, cakes, pastries and biscuits. Cut down on sugar – it supplies energy but no useful nutrients.

You should also cut down on alcohol, which will be good for your general health as well as for cutting calories. For men the sensible limit is no more than twenty-one units a week and for women it's no more than fourteen (one unit of alcohol equals a half pint of beer or a glass of wine or a glass of sherry or a single whisky).

Is crash dieting worthwhile?

I once had a letter from a woman who lost two stone in weight every couple of years by going on a starvation diet. She said that she found she could keep up the starving process for about four weeks. She didn't feel too bad but her friends and colleagues at work often commented that she looked ill. She wanted to know whether she was doing herself any harm by crash dieting.

Well, when you savagely reduce calorie intake, the body's fat stores are mobilized and 'burnt' to provide energy. This process, known as metabolism, can't take place on its own. The metabolism of fat needs a little carbohydrate or protein to keep the 'fire' burning, otherwise the fat collects in the bloodstream, leading to ketosis and potential illness. Ketosis is the condition when fat globules – called ketone bodies – circulate in the blood. They get into this form when there isn't enough carbohydrate available to break them down for use by the body. The body tries to compensate by breaking down its own protein – its muscles, for instance. This can make you feel very weak and ill at first. In the long run, the essential proteins in your blood may not be able to be replenished, causing the swollen feet and ankles and lung congestion observed in the starving refugees of a famine-hit country.

Carbohydrate stores are burnt up in around three days, once starvation begins, so the body starts to 'eat' its own muscles from then on. While that could protect, for example, the starving survivor of a shipwreck until help arrived (the kind of threat the process was designed for), it's not desirable as part of a health-producing diet.

Also, on a starvation diet, the body's mineral balance can become upset. And minerals are necessary for, among other things, the continued and efficient beating of the heart.

Fortunately, most of the time our bodies somehow compensate for the crazy extremes we go to, so no long-term damage is done. But, for safety's sake, it's not wise to lose more than an average of three pounds a week and it's generally not a good idea to go much below the ideal weight for your height, except with professional guidance.

Drastic measures

Some people, in spite of dieting, remain overweight, or even put on weight with a food intake that for most other people would result in weight loss. So, because of the health risks of being overweight, it is essential, if not vital, that someone who is carrying a large quantity of excess weight should be offered help through whatever acceptable techniques there are available.

Stomach stapling is one such extreme. In effect, this treatment – medically known as gastroplasty – makes the entrance to the stomach, as well as the stomach itself, smaller. It's very difficult, if not impossible, once the stomach has been stapled, to eat more than 1000 to 1200 calories a day.

Consuming so few calories will definitely reduce a person's weight, as long as it is rigorously adhered to every day – which it obviously will be if you've had your stomach stapled. However, to exist on much fewer calories for longer than a week or two brings other dangers and is not advisable except under the strict supervision of your doctor or dietician.

Stomach stapling is recommended for only a very small minority of severely overweight people. It is major surgery, after all, and is not without its own risks – complications may include peptic ulceration, vomiting, even a risk of dislodged staples.

Jaw wiring is another extreme means of helping a person to lose weight, but more often than not the person goes back to their old eating habits once the wires are removed, and the weight is therefore put back on. It has the further disadvantage of requiring a near liquid diet, since lumps of food of any size can't be put into the mouth.

Personally, I don't like the idea of this method but then serious problems sometimes demand dramatic measures.

Almost, but not quite, in the same category is the practice of putting a nylon wire around the waistline so that it becomes very uncomfortable if the middle begins to spread. It serves as yet one more reminder that diets are not being observed but can easily be cut off at any point.

Metabolic wards One study has pointed out that out of 400 obese patients, not one failed to lose weight in a metabolic ward, given a diet of 800 calories a day. In such a ward the staff are able to control all the food that the patient receives so that the precise intake is known and there can be no unconscious 'cheating'.

I believe many people who have dieted unsuccessfully may be able to achieve weight loss if they are given realistic targets set over a long-term period. If you are trying to lose weight you do need to bear in mind that you cannot expect pounds to drop off in a week. If you follow a diet of 1000 calories a day you will probably only lose on average just over two pounds a week.

Try to resist the temptation of weighing yourself every day. This can often lead to disappointment and can only serve to make you give up your diet. Weigh yourself just once a week. If you feel you need an element of supervision, it may help to ask if your surgery's nurse could weigh you once a week instead.

If you have tried diets in the past and were unable to stick to them you could try counselling. Understanding why you keep eating so much may help in the long term. The effects of stress can take many forms and, as well as symptoms such as anxiety, lack of concentration, poor sleep and irritability, it can lead to under- as well as over-eating. If you feel your over-eating is triggered by stress you should learn ways of coping with it (see pages 103–5).

If you are fighting obesity there are some self-help rules you can follow. One is don't buy tempting food-stuffs and then store them in the larder. Knowing there is a packet of chocolate biscuits in the cupboard won't help your determination – and the urge to eat *just one* could chip away at your self-discipline! As I say later on, having a little of a food you really like now and then will probably do you more *good* than harm, but try not to snack. Set yourself regular meal times and keep to them. If you're a busy mum, don't nibble at the left-overs on the plates when you're clearing the table. Eat to satisfy your hunger rather than for pleasure, or because you are bored or fed up.

Where you can, use the stairs instead of taking the lift or escalator and walk instead of taking a bus or using the car when the distance is relatively small.

Some people have found they have been able to lose weight by joining a non-medical slimming group, such as Weight Watchers and the like. I remember one woman wrote to me saying she had successfully lost weight through such a group. She had been suffering from obesity for more than twenty years, throughout her married life. She weighed sixteen stone at her heaviest. She had been happily married and had two children, but, she told me, her weight problem had put a strain on her marriage and family life – mainly because of the way she felt about herself. Her work brought her into contact with food, which didn't help her problem either.

I never used to go out because I didn't have any clothes to wear. My husband often used to have work social evenings to go to but I would never go with him. What was the point of trying to get dressed up when all I had to wear was a dress as big as a tent? I never let anyone know what size clothes I had to take. I used to send away for them by mail order. I got so big I even had to sew in extra pieces of elastic into my bras. And to stop anyone finding out what size clothes I took, I used to cut out the labels from my bras and underwear, dresses, cardigans, the lot. I didn't want anyone else to know because I was so ashamed and unhappy.

I was amazed my husband even wanted to be seen out with me. I would stay in night after night. When I was on my own I used to feel so lonely I hated myself and my body. So to make the loneliness go away I began to drink a glass of sherry. As the weeks went by I used to drink more and more, secretly of course.

Family holidays used to bring on terrible loneliness for this woman. Year after year she'd be too ashamed to join in the fun.

We used to go to holiday camps with the children. But I would never join in. I wouldn't go to the entertainments in the evening. I would never, ever allow anyone to take my photograph. I was far too embarrassed. But I was able to get away with this because I made sure I was always the one to take the pictures, or I'd pretend I wanted to go to the loo whenever I saw anyone with the camera. I just couldn't cope with the thought of seeing a photograph of myself.

I would never go on the beach with the family. I felt I was an embarrassment to them. I didn't want to be made fun of either. I used to think that if anyone saw me sitting on the beach looking like a big whale they would just laugh. So no matter what the weather I would sit in the holiday apartment on my own feeling more and more miserable and more and more sorry for myself. Yet I was the only one I could blame for my size and I hated myself even more for that. I felt as if I was in a vicious circle. I'd eat because I was lonely and frustrated, yet I was lonely and frustrated because I used to eat. I knew my size wasn't doing me any good but I just pushed the thought of heart disease to the back of my mind. You always think, 'It'll never happen to me.'

The funny thing was that people used to say to me, 'But you don't eat very much.' And I didn't. Or at least I thought I didn't. I used to work in a fish and chip shop, behind the counter. When I thought about it, all day long I would nibble. It would be just a chip here and there but throughout the day that amounted to a lot. Then, when I went home, I felt that I deserved a big dinner because I'd been out at work all day. So I did consume plenty of calories. And it was all the wrong things – I loved meat pies, lamb chops with lots of fat on them, bacon sandwiches piled high with mayonnaise.

The final trigger to lose weight came when this woman's daughter announced that she was getting married, in two years' time. Determined that she would go to the wedding looking as smartly dressed as any other bride's mother, she joined a local slimming group. There she met other women who were just as overweight as she was. Up until that point she had felt very isolated and guilty. For the next two years or so she dieted conscientiously and sensibly and she found that having such a long-term goal helped her a lot. When she had tried to diet in the past she had always wanted to lose weight *immediately* – when she didn't she would just give up. This time she just wanted to reduce her weight by her two-year deadline. For the wedding she was able to buy the outfit *she wanted*, not the only outfit in the shop that would fit her, she told me joyfully.

Exercise

Another means of aiding weight loss is taking regular exercise. A recent national survey by the Sports Council and the Health Education Authority has revealed that three-quarters of all adults don't take enough exercise. One study showed that obese people rarely exercise intensely enough to cause a prolonged increase in their metabolic rate. Yet exercise keeps you in trim, increases your stamina, helps maintain a healthy heart and is a good means of relieving stress. So it's not just good for helping you lose weight, it's good for your general health too.

But don't push yourself beyond your own limitations. Exercise can mean something as simple as going for a brisk walk or joining a ballroom dancing class. Swimming is also an excellent way of exercising. If you are severely overweight, I would ask your doctor to recommend the best form of exercise for you. Remember, the success of any exercise plan depends on whether you enjoy it. Treat it as a pleasure not a punishment.

So the best way to lose weight is by a combination of sensible dieting and an increase in exercise. There's really no excuse for sitting there doing nothing!

6: WHAT FAMILIES CAN DO TO HELP

Family life can be devastated by eating disorders. Usually everyone wants to help, mothers in particular, but they have no idea what to do or how to behave towards the sufferer.

A serious illness can cause great upset in any family, but one that is hard to understand or accept without in part blaming yourselves can be even more difficult to cope with. People may have vaguely heard of eating disorders such as anorexia or bulimia, but all too often have no real grasp of their true meaning, implication and consequence.

To make matters even worse, it is often the case that the more families try to help, the more rebellious the sufferer becomes. This is because they don't see themselves in the same way that everyone else does – they only see what they want to see. They can resent everyone around them and totally misunderstand the motives for their relatives and friends' well-meaning actions. Despite this, family support and understanding does play an important part in any recovery period.

An anorexic is likely to become depressed, moody, manipulative and very dependent on (although often aggressive towards) her mother. All this makes for someone who is very difficult to live with and understand, and it is no wonder that families of anorexics often become depressed and confused as well as desperately worried.

The families of bulimics have a slightly different set of problems because of the secrecy of the disorder and the sufferer's ability to disguise it. Families and friends may not even realize the sufferer has an eating disorder for quite some time. There can be different degrees of bulimia: from a vomit now and then if they've eaten a particularly big meal, to bulimia in its most severe form. Not everyone who suffers from it has the disorder in its severest form, particularly when the condition is developing.

Stealing from the family or shop lifting can be another consequence of bulimia that can affect everyone. The desire for food may sometimes become so overwhelming that a sufferer will actually steal if they don't have enough money.

As I mentioned earlier, eating disorders can put a great strain on relationships – between parent and child, and between man and wife. I remember receiving a letter from a desperate husband who had just discovered that his wife had bulimia. Up until then, he couldn't understand why their marriage was hitting such a rocky patch. His wife's mood changes were causing terrible tension. One minute she could be very loving, the next extremely aggressive. He was on the point of walking out when he discovered that she had an eating disorder which she had kept hidden from him.

He asked me whether bulimia could have caused her violent mood changes. And yes, they could have. Bulimics can be hard people to live with. Their vomiting can be exhausting, as can the pressure on them to keep the bingeing and vomiting secret. They are almost always ashamed and guilt-ridden about their habits – so they take it out on someone they love. These mood changes can also be a way of distancing people, so that they are left to binge on their own.

So if as a parent or partner or friend you are worried by someone's behaviour and loss of weight, then go to your GP and discuss your fears with him or her. It may be enough simply to get guidelines from the doctor, such as an agreed target weight and a diet sheet, and to arrange for the patient to visit him or her weekly to be weighed and to talk about particular anxieties. All the eating disorders will need to be dealt with in a similar and loving way, but each family approach must be adapted to the individual as much as the condition.

If this seems difficult, perhaps referral to a consultant who specializes in treating anorexia – usually a psychiatrist – may be recommended. He will assess the family situation and in some cases may decide that a spell in hospital is advisable, as I've explained earlier.

If your family member will not admit to having an eating disorder there are tell-tale signs you can look out for if their behaviour is causing you concern. The signs of anorexia are the physical symptoms we talked about earlier. To recap briefly, they include weight loss, continual dieting or eating lots of low-calorie food, fainting, dizzy spells, hair loss or fine, downy hair appearing on the body, and in girls menstrual periods stopping or not developing. Emotional signs include severe mood swings, an obsessive fear of becoming fat, and a compulsion to exercise vigorously.

Tell-tale signs of bulimia can, as I've said, be slightly more difficult to spot. Bulimics will often eat normally if they are sitting at a table eating with other people. Yet you may notice that they don't like to sit still for long once the meal is finished. This could be because they are keen to get away to look for a chance to 'purge' themselves of the food they have consumed. All in secret, of course. You may also notice food disappearing from the kitchen.

The physical signs include loss of tooth enamel, a puffy face (due to swollen salivary glands), even epileptic fits in some cases. Marks on the backs of fingers are another sign to look for, caused when the sufferer makes themselves vomit.

What are the signs of a compulsive eater? Well, mainly knowing that the person cannot possibly be hungry, yet they still want to eat. They may become quiet and withdrawn after eating a lot of food because they feel guilty. They may like to eat foods that are high in sugar and/or carbohydrates, and if, as is likely, the eating compulsion takes place in secret, then weight gain will appear even though they seem to be eating very little.

A word of advice if you suspect you have a family member suffering from an eating disorder. *There's no point lecturing.* What a sufferer very often needs most is to be listened to. It can help you if you read everything you can about eating disorders. Discovering the experiences of other sufferers, as well as their families, can be rewarding and enlightening, which is why I have included case studies in this book and suggested that you attend a self-help group meeting.

For anorexics, you need to encourage eating; for bulimics and compulsive eaters, you need to establish a regular eating pattern. For someone who is very overweight, you will need to give encouragement and support. For example, if they are trying to cut down on chocolate, don't eat a bar in front of them!

Keeping a diary has helped sufferers too (see page 109). You could help in compiling this, as well as giving the sufferer encouragement and support to fill it in on their own.

Making mealtimes a battleground – for an anorexic by wanting her to eat high-calorie food, or for a compulsive eater by wanting her to eat low-calorie food – can be disastrous. The family meal should be an enjoyable affair. It should be a time when everyone can get together and talk, as well as eat, rather than a time when you all eat quickly and silently while staring at the television.

Fathers shouldn't leave everything to the mothers. It's important that, even though there may be work pressures, you spend time with your family. You need to show your child that you support them no matter what their academic achievements, and help them accept that you care for them for what they are. And it's hard, I know, not to fall into the trap of putting all your energy into your anorexic child or bulimic partner, but if you have other family members take care not to 'neglect' them.

A few parents of anorexics may realize that they, too, don't really want their child to grow up. I've heard parents, particularly mums, say that they are anxious about their young leaving home because it will create an emotional gap, as well as anxiety about how they will cope in the big world. But we all have to let go. Don't think you are in any way abnormal if you feel this way sometimes. If you have found that you are frightened of being left alone and are anxious about letting go, you could seek counselling help.

Counselling can be good for everyone involved. When self-esteem and self-confidence is low, and you and your family seem not to be in charge of your lives, the help of an expert who can look at what's going on and at the choices you can make, is often invaluable. Helping people to identify their fears, work through them and feel more positive about their actions or decisions can in time prove very successful.

Don't be frightened to let your son or daughter's school know that you are anxious that he or she may have an eating disorder. Teachers there may well have experience in dealing with other cases and, not only that, they might have already suspected that your son or daughter has the beginnings of the problem anyway.

One counsellor, who has helped many eating dis-order sufferers, told me that one of the most important things to stress to a mother, father or friend, and one of the most difficult to carry out day after day, is just to be there. Of course, just being there can be very difficult for a carer – often they are on the receiving end of much abuse. The sufferer's reactions to help can vary so much from day to day: some days they may want to be helped and to cling on to your advice, other days they may be totally resentful of your 'interference'. And all too often the carer is inclined to say they've had enough and can't cope. But no matter how difficult it becomes, do try to hang on in there. You may not be thanked now, but you will be one day.

Trying to understand how a sufferer is feeling and why they are behaving in this way is also an important aspect of treatment. I believe that talking about self-help measures is important for encouraging sufferers, first of all, to admit to themselves that they have a problem and, secondly, to encourage them to do something about it. This can be a very frightening thing for sufferers to face because they need their eating disorders to be over-whelming and to occupy their thoughts constantly for in that way the disorder can be their security blanket. Life without such a 'comforter' can be more frightening than day-to-day living with the eating disorder itself.

We talk about self-help groups in more detail on page 97, as many sufferers gain great benefit from this means of therapy. It may help if you point out to the sufferer that they don't need to go alone, a member of the family could accompany them, or a trusted friend.

It's important for family members both to talk and to listen. It may help sufferers to discuss the things that are upsetting them and you need to listen well, even if you have heard it all before.

Information can be of great benefit. Knowing the basic facts can help everyone involved put things into perspective. Read as much as you can about the subject of eating disorders and, as I've said, even go along to a self-help group so that you can listen to the experience of others. It's not unusual for a daughter to accompany an anorexic mother, or for a husband to accompany a wife. It is so difficult for someone to appreciate why a person is refusing to eat, or why they are bingeing and purging, when you do not understand what eating disorders are all about. It's so easy to think, naïvely, that eating disorders are about food. But as one counsellor states, 'The eating isn't the disorder. The eating is the sufferer's solution to the problem. They are using food as a way of coping with a problem they don't want to address.'

Trying to get to grips with the logic behind eating disorders can be hard. A father once contacted the *Jimmy Young Show* to ask me why his daughter couldn't stop bingeing or taking laxatives. He had a good enough relationship to be able to talk things through with her, and she had admitted that she knew her erratic eating habits were not doing her body any good. She told him week after week that now she was strong enough to be able to stop, that she really wanted to stop. But despite promising these things to herself and to him, the bingeing and purging continued. And he just couldn't understand why.

But bulimic behaviour can be addictive. Vomiting can make a sufferer want to over-eat all over again. It can also set up cravings for more of the same food. The Eating Disorders Association likens sufferers to heroin addicts in their addiction to self-abuse as a means of problem-solving. The heroin addict first takes the drug as a means of pleasure or to seek refuge from troubles, but is then gripped by the drug as it takes control both mentally and physically.

ADOLESCENCE

I receive so many letters about being a parent, I often think it's a shame we don't have parenting lessons at secondary school dealing with the handling of teenage problems. It would certainly benefit the parents of the pupils! Both sides don't seem to be able to understand each other or their respective problems – and the teen-age years can be an emotional minefield for everyone involved. I do feel, though, that I ought to give parents a little encouragement. Apparently studies have now revealed that most teenagers *actually do like* their parents and feel that they get on well with them. You would never have guessed, would you?

It's not too difficult to see why the emotional storms of the adolescent years take place. The adult hormones are starting to flow, causing growth and change in the most sensitive parts of the body. Sexual desire, often present before, in any case – hence the 'crushes' at primary schools – now becomes even stronger. The growth spurt makes the child look like an adult in the space of a couple of years and the opinions and views of your peers suddenly become far more important than those of your parents. Hence the emotional, physical and social turmoil that hits early teenagers.

Because of all the rapid physical changes taking place – spots, pubic hair, developing breasts and periods in girls, or having to shave and the voice breaking in boys – teenagers can become particularly self-conscious and will need reassurance that they are just the same as everyone else. Two of the most regular letters I get are from teenagers: the girls assume that they are grossly abnormal because they have started to get perfectly normal vaginal discharges, and the boys because they think their penis is abnormally small.

Both say that they feel they will never be able to have a normal sex life and family because of their 'disability'. Over the past twenty years the words they use have hardly changed and deep anxiety screams from every line. They daren't tell anyone face-to-face, except an agony aunt or uncle. What is even more sad is that they believe, and tell me, that they are the only ones in the world to whom this is happening!

A self-conscious teenager, particularly one who has weight problems, will be even more sensitive about the comments of others. Teasing can lead them to believe that they are not likeable as people. For some teenagers this consciousness of their body results in dieting or over-eating – factors which can all lead to the development of an eating disorder.

The Royal College of Psychiatrists points out research that has shown that, at some time, four out of ten adolescents have felt so miserable that they've cried and have wanted to get away from everyone and everything. At some point in the course of their adolescence more than one in five think so little of themselves that life does not seem worth living. All these feelings of uncertainty can lead to real emotional distress.

Above all, parents, do not blame yourselves. There is no point feeling responsible for the way your child has developed or faced growing up. As the Eating Disorders Association advises, parents usually do what they think is best at the time, and everyone can be wise in retrospect. Accept what has happened in the past and concentrate on what can be done now and in the future.

Jenny Caesar, who runs BANISH, a self-help group in the Lancashire area, believes that dealing with a sufferer in the family can be like treading on glass. 'You have to remember that the sufferers themselves really don't like themselves. And you have to help get them to like or love themselves as a person – until you do that you can't get them to turn the eating problem around,' she says.

She warns that you have to be very careful about the things you say to a sufferer of an eating disorder and that it is very important to think before you speak. 'To say to them something like not eating or eating too much is "a stupid thing to do" is hopeless. An average person could brush off a comment like that quite easily. But a sufferer can take it personally and actually genuinely begin to believe that they are stupid. They have such low self-confidence that we have to tell sufferers that if their opinion is different or not the same as everyone else's that doesn't mean that it's wrong. You can only make them like themselves by getting them to look at how they see things. But it can be really difficult to know what to say. To say something like "you look well" means to them that they look fat. For families it's like treading on glass.

'I feel sorry for parents because it's so rare for them to say the right thing. It can be terrifying because sufferers are so sensitive it's unreal. They can read anything they want into a comment. If someone asks them whether or not they watched a certain television programme the night before, such a simple question can cause trouble. Instead of just saying that they didn't, they will wonder *why* they didn't. They can turn sentences around and use them as a weapon against themselves.'

Jenny believes that part of the problem often faced by people with eating disorders is that they have very high standards of their own. They seem to think that everyone else automatically has similarly high standards, and when people inevitably don't, they turn the inadequacy back on themselves. 'If they have a bad relationship they automatically think it's their fault. They put a lot of their own standards on to other people: if they put so much into a relationship, they don't understand why the other person can't put so much back.

'You can help by encouraging the sufferer to believe that you don't need to be perfect in this world. But that can take a lot of convincing. It can take much time and patience on the part of the family too. When you break down the fact that they don't need to be perfect you're really breaking down the walls and getting somewhere.'

Another useful approach is pointing out that their lives aren't actually any better when they are thin or bingeing. 'Convincing them of this is, of course, very difficult,' says Jenny. 'When they examine it themselves they may see that life isn't much different. They try to convince themselves that they are happy. In a way it's a withdrawal from the world. People start to tiptoe around them and so most of the responsibilities of day-to-day living are taken away from them. They then don't have the average person's worries, in my opinion, like paying the electricity bill or whatever.

'They are hurt inside. For example, a sufferer can have a bad marriage. Now whereas most people will fight to try to save it or give up and get a divorce, sufferers will sit it out and close off all their feelings so they don't have to think about it. They tend to put a fence around themselves so no one can hurt them. They don't like to show their emotions and try to portray that they can cope with anything. But deep down they are sad and lonely.

'They may not know the motives for their behaviour, but I believe all sufferers have their own genuine reasons. The problem may be tiny to you but to them it's overwhelming – it could be something like a girl worrying about her virginity or just what sort of clothes to buy. And you have to remember that some are terrified of finding out why they feel the way they do.'

CASE STUDY: DEBBIE

Debbie Lovell, a twenty-three-year-old psychology Ph.D. student who has written a book about her own experience called Hungry for Love, suffered from anorexia from the age of sixteen to eighteen and believes that families should learn to show their feelings and their love.

There were a number of triggers for my anorexia – self-hatred and being bullied at school, so I had low self-esteem. It was around exam time so stress was involved and it was the time of Ethiopian families being shown on television. I felt that I didn't deserve food because those people were starving. Teenage friends were also dieting. Dieting gave me a feeling of control. I had an overprotective mother who chose what I should wear and what time I should be in at night. Here was one area where I had control. My dad was a marathon runner and I would run with him. By losing weight to look like a slim runner I thought I was pleasing him and the family.

Once it started it kept going. It perpetuated itself. My stomach had shrunk and it was then painful when I did eat. I could forget about my problems by thinking what I was going to eat or what I was not going to eat.

As a family we had tried to be perfect, and it seemed there were no problems. My family first put down my weight loss to the running and the exams. We all tried to pretend it wasn't 'a problem'. When I collapsed we thought that it was diabetes rather than admit it was psychological.

The best part of a year had gone by before Debbie received help.

My mother was interested but I was lying to her about food. I would make excuses about not eating or lie that I had had a big school lunch. I did try hard to cover it up. But my advice to sufferers and families is find someone to talk about it to. Be willing to be honest with the person involved. Be willing to talk about your own concerns. Go on loving and accepting the sufferer.

When we all realized there was a problem I went into hospital for eight weeks and my parents were wonderful. They came to see me every day. We had never hugged or showed any emotions and suddenly they showed how much they cared. They showed me that they loved me for what I was and not for what I could do – I had thought I had to be perfect. I remember coming home from school once saying that I had got 98 per cent in a mock O level exam, and I was asked what had happened to the other 2 per cent. I felt I had to get top marks all the time.

Debbie's experience of family therapy was also beneficial.

It really helped us all, by making us talk about our feelings. During the first session my mother cried. I'd never seen her cry before. We had bottled our feelings up. There were never rows or emotions shown in our family. My mother is overweight and she would stuff all the feelings down with food and I would starve. We even used to eat in different rooms. The therapist advised us to sit down together once a week for a meal. By doing this we sat, we talked, got to know each other and the meal became enjoyable too.

We were very nervous about the sessions. We didn't want the family to be put under the microscope, especially as we had spent years pretending to be a perfect family and now there was the stigma that we needed to get help and that we had a problem. The sessions helped us to stop pretending to be perfect and be more real with each other. It's important for parents to show emotions to children, to be honest about everything, instead of pretending that things are perfect. They should be honest about how they are feeling, that there are good days and bad days and show that it's OK to be angry sometimes.

Debbie also has advice for friends, as well as family.

If an anorexic is putting on weight, don't tell her that she looks better. Comment on anything other than her appearance. Say things like, 'You seem to have a lot more confidence these days' or 'It's great that you are going out a lot more.' Try to focus attention on the fact that it's not appearance that matters. Try to talk about other things rather than food or appearance.

I know that friends don't know what to do. An eating disorder tends to make you isolated. I felt I was an awful person and that I didn't deserve friends. I thought I was spoiling their time. But I would say to friends, keep being there for the person and show that you do want to spend time with them. Do ring them up. Do call round to see them on the off-chance. Try to help them talk about the underlying problem. Don't be frightened to ask, to show that you care.

7: SELF-HELP TREATMENT

To put yourself on the road to recovery, you must first own up to the fact that you have an eating disorder. I remember receiving a letter from a woman who said that she had started bingeing and vomiting, as well as taking laxatives, when her husband left her for a younger woman. Up until then her eating patterns had been normal. She wrote to me because she didn't know where to turn for help. But by writing she was taking the first step towards recovery, because she had admitted to herself that she had a problem that needed to be dealt with. Wanting advice is a positive step.

And this is true of anorexia, bulimia, compulsive eating and obesity. Of course, the sooner you recognize you have a problem, the sooner you are likely to overcome it. Refusing to admit you need help only means that you suffer longer and consequently recovery will take more time and your health will be put at greater risk.

Genevieve Blais, a psychotherapist and herself a recovered anorexic and compulsive eater, has strong ideas about how you can help yourself. In her opinion, one of the most important traps to avoid is wanting to diet.

'Dieting sets people up to gain weight and sets women in a cycle of failure from which they can't possibly break out. Dieting chips away at women's self-esteem. As soon as they eat normally they'll regain all the weight lost through a diet. Compulsive eating, for example, is not a simple matter. You really have to look at and treat the whole person.'

Another important aspect of coming to terms with

your own body is talking about 'realism'. There's no point looking at a copy of *Vogue* and thinking that if you diet you'll look like one of the models inside. Learning to accept that you are the shape and bone structure that you are and that no matter what shape you are you're still a worthwhile person is vital.

'You have to cover genetic realities,' insists Genevieve. 'You're led to believe that if you diet you are going to have a different body, almost, for example, that if you diet long enough you are going to have long slim legs.'

Genevieve also believes that it is important to look at what she calls the physics of food and also to look back over your life to understand yourself and work out where your habits and eating behaviour came from. You need to examine your relationship with your parents – but, says Genevieve, remember that there aren't any perfect parents, and children have their own personalities.

'Everybody's body is unique and we all respond differently to food. Our body chemistry changes every seven years – allergies can come and go, for instance. Food is very important because it can affect you on a physical and emotional level. So you have to look at the physics of food and work out how particular foods make you feel and how that food reacts with you. Learning about what we put in our bodies is important.

'So is working out how you see the world and how you see yourself. You have to connect the dots. The idea is not to blame your parents, it's not that simple. We are all individual personalities and we all have to take responsibility for our own actions at some point. You need to question where you got your ideas about life, then decide what's true for you.

'No habit is necessary. Behaviour patterns are learned and they can be relearned. Most people don't examine where their eating patterns came from, they just react to them. But if you don't like some of your behaviour patterns you have to realize that you are not locked into them. It is so important that people know it's possible to recover – it does take energy and determination. People don't have to suffer the way they do. They have to see that they have created their own suffering.'

Like Genevieve, I do believe that if we don't examine our feelings, and keep our anger or our loneliness or our emotional needs or whatever, suppressed, this will take its toll on our mental well-being and, through eating disorders, eventually on our physical health. But while examining your feelings you have to realize that whatever happened to you in the past is now over. You are in charge of your own life, your own destiny, so to speak. *Nobody else.* You and *you alone* must make decisions about your life and the way you behave.

In my opinion, learning to like yourself and learning to respect yourself are essential steps towards recovery. There's nothing sadder than hearing an ordinary person say that they hate themselves, or that they have deserved their unhappy childhood or bad treatment by men. Everybody is equal and everybody is entitled to happiness.

LEARNING TO OPEN UP

Joining a self-help group can be extremely rewarding for many sufferers and often preferable to seeking psychiatric help because of the stigma attached to it. One self-help group leader told me, 'At a group meeting sufferers can really share where they are at. Anorexics, bulimics and over-eaters can be a mixture of people doing different things, but the underlying reasons are often very similar. One person tends to start talking, then someone comes in with a supporting comment. Their big worry is usually eating – either they are eating too much or not eating at all. They don't ask us direct questions but talk around the issues underlying the problem. A lot of them say that they don't know what the cause of the problem is. But just talking between themselves and off-loading to someone who knows how they feel is so helpful to them, which is why they come back to the meetings. They know there is going to be somebody there who knows exactly how they are feeling.'

Sally Israel, a counsellor at a Cardiff self-help group, firmly believes that for many sufferers self-help is the best form of treatment. I think so too because, when it works, you feel that you've managed to get over it in a non-medical, non-medicinal way. It makes you feel, 'I'm in control and with a bit of friendly help, I got through it.'

'We normally get people who come to the group because they tried the doctor first – doctors in Cardiff tend to know about our group. Or, they would go to a psychiatrist and not get on very well, then they have gone back to their GP who has suggested they join the group. Or women are referred to us through local hospitals.

'The facilitators are all ex-sufferers. With something like eating disorders it takes someone who has suffered it to really understand what the person is going through. Nothing they say or do will shock us. Some of them do some "dirty" or "disgusting" things – as they describe it – with food. These could be throwing up in a carrier bag, or throwing up in a lane, or going into every burger store in town then throwing up in an alley. Things that sufferers consider barbaric.'

Sally believes that for a self-help group to be successful and not scare sufferers away, the atmosphere needs to be relaxed and unpressurized. Sufferers shouldn't be made to feel that they must join in, or that they have to reveal their innermost feelings. For some, simply listening to the experience of others can be very rewarding and encouraging.

'We don't pressurize anyone into talking. We open the group with a theme or topic, such as body image, relationships with parents, *et cetera*. We try to set an exercise – perhaps five minutes thinking about the topic, or writing something down – but nothing to do with food. We might ask them to think of all the good things about their eating disorder or all the bad things. We try to put members in touch with their emotions. They may say: "A good thing is that I can eat as many chocolate bars as I want." We then try to relate the feelings with the food.

'We see the food as a result of these feelings. We try to get them to think why they are eating the way they are and what was happening in their lives before they had the disorder. And mainly how they are coping at the moment, if there is something that is triggering off a binge.

'It's a very relaxed group and we are subtle in our approach. We don't make people feel we are probing, asking them questions or challenging them.'

I know from the letters I've received that for many sufferers – not only of eating disorders, but a wide range of conditions from arthritis to migraine – meeting other sufferers has been a turning point in coming to terms with their problem. Sally agrees.

'For many people an eating disorder is such an isolated thing, it's a relief for them to walk into a room and meet twelve other women who are doing the same things as them. They feel they can talk about themselves as they never have before. It's amazing how many phone calls we have from women who say that they don't know whether they are going to come, or whether the group will help – then the first week they come they soon settle down and are very relaxed.'

Despite the success of self-help groups in general, many sufferers don't know of their existence. 'I believe self-help groups need a lot of publicity,' Sally points out. 'We've been running the Cardiff one for four years and we can't do any more. There is a terrific demand for what we do. Some women travel fifteen or twenty miles to the group – they are the lucky ones who have a car.

'Yet self-help is such an important form of treatment. I believe the worst form of treatment is in hospital, un-less obviously the problem has become life-threatening. Of course, the best form of treatment is different for different women. Some women find private counselling as well as going to a group, some have found a good therapist and psychologist. But I'm sure a self-help group or counselling is the most beneficial.

'In my experience I've found that the majority of women have been incredibly dissatisfied with the psychi-atric system. They feel they're seen for fifteen minutes once a fortnight, weighed and given a diet sheet and that's about it.'

If you do decide a self-help group is for you, please don't expect a miracle cure. Getting over an eating dis-order can take a long time. The longer you have been entrenched in a way of living, the longer it can take for you to develop a different lifestyle. As Sally says, 'It takes years to recover from an eating disorder and years to put your trust in someone. We have to reassure women all the time that recovery is possible. It may feel as if you take three steps backwards and one forward. After coming to the group some women end up feeling worse and so their eating disorder gets worse. But we say, stay with it.'

The first few meetings of a self-help group can produce frightening reactions in many people. Although they may feel relaxed in the company of other sufferers, they are at last confronting the problems or the causes of what led them to develop the eating disorder.

'Suddenly talking about all these feelings can be very confusing – especially when they have been squashed and then they're brought to the surface. Bulimics put down their feelings, anorexics don't want feelings at all, and compulsive eaters are very needy – they eat and eat but they can't get enough and they can't get fulfilled.

'So it takes a very long time. To begin with the feelings are all out of proportion. So although it may feel as though they are going backwards what is important is that they are beginning to feel and that they are learning to cope with their feelings. It's going to take time but we have seen it work. We've had women of fifty plus who've been bulimic for say twenty or more years without ever telling a soul. Then perhaps an eighteen-year-old who's been bulimic for two or three years. But remember, you can recover.'

A self-help group can also help those who are severely overweight. Obese people have found it helpful to join a group such as Weight Watchers (see the case history of pages 76–8). They can find the mutual support in such a group gives them the encouragement they need to carry on reducing their food intake. After all, often their problem has taken years to build up and it can take many months, if not years, for it to disappear. Self-help groups are ideal for those who prefer to deal with people from a non-medical background, and, as they are under no obligation to keep going back, there is no pressure.

CASE STUDY: ELISE

Like Sally, Elise who is twenty-five and has had anorexia for eight years, believes self-help groups are invaluable.

> I developed anorexia for several reasons. I was always striving to be perfect. My family is middle-class, and found it very hard to show love. I got love by achieving. I worked hard to get good grades, but then found another way of achieving – through cutting down on food.

Elise has been through many desperate times and her weight once dropped to five stone. When her weight was low she felt dreadful.

> I wasn't really of this world. I couldn't wear shoes because they were too heavy for my feet. It was difficult to concentrate or focus my mind on anything. I had blackouts. I found movement difficult. It was painful even to straighten out.

Elise became so ill that help was forced upon her, but she believes you can only truly help a person with an eating disorder when they are ready to be helped.

> One thing about anorexia is having self-respect and having control over your life. Self-help is important in any eating disorder. A person going to a self-help group is making their own choice rather than being taken somewhere for help to be forced upon them. Talking to people who have suffered from similar problems is helpful. They understand why you do what you do. People on the outside think anorexia, for example, is a selfish illness. But the key thing is that it makes the person feel so guilty. Learning from other sufferers that it's not your fault, and that it's an illness, helps take that guilt away. The guilt is so damaging. It makes you lose your self-respect.
>
> Self-help is no good to someone who doesn't want it. You just won't listen. An eating disorder is a state of mind.

It's not what you do or how you do it, it's about how you feel about yourself. At times I found losing weight rewarding and I would enjoy showing off my success to people at the group. I was proud of my thin body. If you go to a group with that state of mind it's not fair to other sufferers. My body was my secret trophy of self-denial.

When the time is right I think self-help is incredible. I was never judged there. I'm ashamed of my problem but there I was listened to and accepted for what I was. I would advise people not to give up. Keep going even if you think it's not for you. It's a haven.

LEARNING HOW TO DEAL WITH STRESS

Stress can trigger the very first beginnings of an eating disorder. It can lead those who already have an eating disorder to starve themselves, or it can cause binges leading to bulimia and compulsive eating. Compulsive eating may seem to make the sufferer feel better in the short term, but long term it only adds to their problems.

Measuring stress can be difficult. Stress to one person may not be stress to another, and some of us are naturally more sensitive to it than others. Yet when we have too much stress in our lives we can create all manner of problems for ourselves. Of course, it's not always possible to remove stress factors as they affect us all every day, and from all the letters and calls I receive on the *Jimmy Young Programme* I've realized that recognizing we're stressed – and why – isn't easy for anyone. It can be hard for many people just to admit that they feel stressed – so often it's viewed as a sign of weakness, or of not being able to do one's job properly, or a confession of loneliness.

However, stress isn't always a bad thing. Positive stress, or pressure, is required for us to work well and to drive us to make the most out of life. That rush of adrenalin stimulates and motivates and without it our lives would feel boring and mundane.

I'm sure many readers have heard of the fight or flight response of cavemen. Our bodies have an automatic response to fear or pleasure, releasing the hormones adrenalin and noradrenalin. These cause the heart rate to increase as well as providing instant energy by causing sugars and fats to be released into the blood. As cavemen we would stay and fight the man or animal causing us stress, or we would run away. Not very practical reactions these days! So because we can't 'flee' or 'fight', the body's adrenalin is bottled up instead.

You may not realize when you are under stress, however. Symptoms can include tense muscles, headaches or palpitations. Your breathing can suddenly get faster and you may take many short breaths. You can get sweaty palms and feel restless, tense or exhausted. Your sleeping patterns can change – whereas once you slept well, you now wake up at intervals throughout the night or find that you keep waking early. You may constantly think of things that have happened in the past, times when you have been hurt, and you may suffer from hypochondria, a fear of being seriously ill. These are just a few of the many examples of the symptoms of stress.

The Health Education Authority suggests some simple ways to help you cope with stress. One suggestion is to organize your time by making a list of what is most and what is least urgent. Do things in that order and don't take on more work than you can cope with.

Another suggestion is to make time for relaxing. You can learn this simple relaxation technique: when you know you're unlikely to be disturbed for half an hour or so, sit or lie down where it's comfortable. Let your body sink right down into what's supporting it. Then tense and relax each part of the body in turn – paying attention to any muscles that feel tense. By the time you have worked through all your muscles you will feel as if you're a rag doll. Then go through all your relaxed muscles, thinking about how each one feels so that you learn to recognize when the muscles are becoming tense during a stressful time.

Another good way of reducing stress is to look at your lifestyle as if you were a fly on the wall. And remember, taking control of your life means dealing with one problem at a time.

Sometimes it's easier for someone on the outside to work out what's causing you stress, which is why it's worth listening to the opinion of someone you trust.

Talking about what might be worrying you or what worried you in the past is another good way of coping with stress. Talking through our emotional problems can be the first step towards dealing with them. Naturally, you may prefer to talk to a trained therapist or counsellor, but sometimes just talking to a friend can help. A problem shared is so often a problem halved – it may be an old saying but I think there's value in it!

It's so important for you to realize that you don't have to cope on your own and that if you keep whatever's troubling you to yourself, the shame and guilt involved in keeping it hidden will only reinforce the problem. I firmly believe that facing up to your problems and talking about them is a sign of strength not weakness – a sign of strength that you will allow yourself to seek and accept care and advice from others.

LEARNING HOW TO COPE WITH DEPRESSION

Depression can vary enormously in its severity and in the form it takes. It can be a difficult condition for a person to come to terms with, especially when friends and family, who do not realize that it is a medical condition, are not particularly sympathetic and believe the sufferer should just 'snap out of it'.

When depression in its proper sense develops, the sufferer needs medical help. They may need counselling from a skilled professional. Just as with stress, talking to a person who is sympathetic and able to listen can achieve a cure if the patient is able to unburden themselves and learn to understand why he or she is depressed. Feelings have to be worked through before any moves can be made towards re-establishing a happy and fulfilling life.

Depending on the severity of the depression and your circumstances, your doctor may decide you need anti-depressants and possibly counselling. These are useful and effective drugs for depression – even though, according to MIND, the National Association for Mental Health, they have no useful effect whatsoever for about three depressed people in every ten. And each year about 400 people use anti-depressant drugs as the means to end their lives. Yet these drugs are the most common form of treatment and they do enable many thousands of people to lead worthwhile lives. Anti-depressants are non-addictive and work by acting on chemical processes in the brain – effectively changing a person's sensitivity to emotions.

Even if you are receiving medical treatment there are still self-help measures you can take to cope with depression better. The Royal College of Psychiatrists has six pointers for dealing with depression.

■ Don't bottle things up – having a good cry is part of the mind's natural healing mechanism. Crying releases the body's endorphins, those natural salves of pain, both physical and emotional. A good cry probably does as much as a prescription and it's an ideal way of dealing with stress. Allowing yourself the right to cry is important for many people who suffer from eating disorders. So often they feel they have to present a wonderful image to the outside world – an image of being able to cope with any and every situation.

■ When you feel down *do something*. Go out for a walk, read a book, do some housework. Divert your mind in some way.

■ Eat a good, balanced diet.

■ Resist the temptation to drown your sorrows. Alcohol may give you an immediate lift, but it only depresses your mood in the end.

■ Don't get into a state about not sleeping. The worst thing you can do is lie in bed thinking about the fact that you can't sleep. Depression is a common cause of sleeplessness. Listening to the radio at night, or even watching television, still means that you are resting.

■ Do remind yourself that you are suffering from a medical condition and that it can be treated. Psychiatrists call depression and anxiety 'affective disorders' – both affect the way we feel and will alter our mood.

LEARNING TO EAT HEALTHILY

As I've said throughout this book, eating disorders aren't really about food, they are about people wanting to have control over their lives. However, I do feel I should give some attention here to healthy eating. For all of us, regular eating patterns are essential – whether we have an eating disorder or not. A healthy eating plan should reduce the quantity of refined convenience foods. Fresh fruit and vegetables should be eaten every day, along with small quantities of animal products, including eggs, dairy produce and fish. You should aim for foods rich in vitamins, minerals and fibre and low in added chemicals, fats and too much sugar.

But don't deny yourself any of your 'forbidden' foods – for example, cutting out chocolate altogether. Or, if you have bulimia and tend to binge on, say, chocolate biscuits, make sure you include one or two in your diet. This will be frightening, but by eating them you will be able to prove to yourself that your eating habits are slowly being kept under control. The same goes for someone who is overweight and who adores fried bread, for example. Eat some now and again rather than cutting it out altogether. Denying yourself everything you enjoy will only make it more likely that your healthy eating regime will fail.

Once you're over the worst, don't worry too much about getting down to exactly the right weight for your height. For the mathematically minded, you could keep within the range suggested by the Ponderal or Body Mass Index, which I believe is one of the best guides of all because it encompasses the big/small bone variation as well as your frame size and demonstrates what are considered to be the upper and lower limits of your ideal weight.

You calculate it like this: find out your weight in kilograms and your height in metres. Divide the weight by the height squared, as shown in the following equation:

$$\frac{\text{weight (kg)}}{\text{height (m)}^2} = \text{Body Mass Index}$$

The answer should be between 20 and 25.

KEEPING A FOOD DIARY

Sufferers of all types of eating disorder should try to keep an emotional/food diary. By noting how you felt, how you reacted to situations and what you ate, or how a situation made you not want to eat, may be helpful in coming to terms with and understanding what is triggering the continuation of your disorder. It could be really helpful by highlighting that you do have good days, when you don't binge or vomit or take laxatives, for example. Use your diary as a source of encouragement. Don't be frightened to confront in detail the reasons for your eating behaviour, or frightened to find out what the triggers are for your bingeing or starving. By discovering these triggers you may be able to avoid them the next time, or be able to confront them without resorting to food for comfort.

Keeping a food diary can be helpful in beating obesity, as well as the other disorders. You may be able to trace a pattern of when eating is just out of habit or one of your rituals. This can then help you to break any habits you may have formed over the years. Frequently many people have no idea that they are eating excess amounts purely from habit.

Also, there's always the general suggestion, usually made more in hope than anticipation, that the sufferer should take up an absorbing hobby! Regrettably, this is a bit like saying, 'Shake yourself out of it.' If the sufferer could shake herself out of it or get involved in an all-absorbing hobby, the problem would of course be much easier to tackle, but it's not as straightforward as that. Still, if the hobby sought was all-absorbing, it would boost the sufferer's sense of identity and self-worth, so I am going to suggest it in any case. The only people who fail in life, as in 'therapy', are those who give up, so give a new hobby, or even a new job, a try!

YES, YOU CAN RECOVER

Admitting you have an eating disorder is a step towards recovery. Seeking professional help, attending a self-help group and then looking at areas of your life you may be unhappy with – and then deciding to do something about them – are all ways of making progress.

As a result of the increased media attention on eating disorders, the conditions are becoming slightly easier to talk about, which helps a sufferer feel less isolated. It may lead her to accept that she really isn't the odd one out and, hopefully, to be less ashamed of her problem. I'm not saying that an eating disorder is socially acceptable, but more bulimics, for example, seem to be facing up to their problems and are having the courage to ask for help.

And courage is so important. From other people, sufferers need compassion and understanding. From themselves, they need courage – the courage to seek help.

HELPFUL ADDRESSES

UNITED KINGDOM

BANISH (Bulimia and Anorexia Nervosa Intermediate Self-Help), 27 Lawrence Avenue, Lytham St Ann's, Lancashire FY8 3LG.

A self-help group for sufferers in the Lancashire area. For information sheets, send an SAE and £1 to Jenny Caesar at the above address.

British Association for Counselling, 1 Regent Place, Rugby CV21 2PJ. Telephone: 0788 578328.

Provides details of counsellors near you, their specialized areas of work and their fees (if any).

Coping Together. Telephone: 0642 217399.

A self-help group for sufferers in the Cleveland area.

Eating Disorders Association, Sackville Place, 44 Magdalen Street, Norwich, Norfolk NR3 1JE.

The association provides support for families and friends as well as sufferers. Most families find it helpful to talk with other families in a similar situation. Many of the association's self-help groups run separate meetings for relatives and friends.

The association has recently merged with the **Society for Advancement of Research into Anorexia (SARA)** and is now trying to promote research into anorexia and bulimia by raising money, asking its members to participate in research and organizing conferences.

The telephone lines enable you to talk to an experienced counsellor. The phone lines can be very busy – in the past as many as 2000 calls each week have been unable to get through. If you have difficulty, please keep trying. Telephone: 0603 621414 (a helpline open Monday–Friday, 9 a.m.–6.30 p.m.) If you're under eighteen you can contact the Youth Helpline on 0603 765050 on Monday, Tuesday and Wednesday between 4–6 p.m. If you ring you will be called back immediately by a helpline worker. You can also obtain information about the charity and anorexia and bulimia by listening to a recorded message on 0336 420568.

The association can also give you the names of private centres or clinics for treating eating disorders in your area, as well as counsellors throughout the country.

Exploring Parenthood.
Telephone: 081 960 1678.

A parents' help and advice line which can put you in touch with qualified counsellors.

The Mental Health Foundation,
37 Mortimer Street, London W1N 7RJ.
Telephone: 071 580 0145.

The foundation is Britain's leading grant-making charity, concerned with promoting and encouraging pioneering research and community care projects in the field of mental health and disorder.

The foundation aims to prevent mental disorders by funding and encouraging research into the causes of mental illness and mental handicap and to improve the quality of life for the mentally disordered by funding and supporting pioneering and innovative care schemes. It produces a series of self-help leaflets such as *Seeing a Psychiatrist*. For a copy, write sending an SAE.

MIND, 22 Harley Street, London W1N 2ED.
Telephone: 071 637 0741.

Publishes a wide range of literature on all aspects of mental health, including eating problems.

Over-eaters Anonymous,
PO Box 19, Stretford, Manchester, M32 9EB.

A self-help group based along the lines of Alcoholics Anonymous. Groups are open to sufferers of eating disorders.

For details of your nearest meeting ring 071 498 5505 where you will hear a recorded message telling you of a contact who covers your area. Or write to the above address.

Parentline.
Telephone: 0628 757077

A confidential helpline for parents to offload problems about their children. The central telephone line is open every weekday from 9 a.m–6 p.m. Callers are given the telephone number and opening hours of the nearest Parentline group.

Parent Link Network,
44–46 Caversham Road, London NW5 2DS.
Telephone: 071 485 8535.

Parent Link offers a listening ear to parents and a chance to learn how to cope with living with teenagers. A Parent Link group begins as twelve weekly sessions and may have up to twelve participants. A session focuses on a particular topic and includes exercises in twos and threes, and small and large group discussions, to explore the topics and help participants practise doing things differently in their families.

The Royal College of Psychiatrists,
17 Belgrave Square, London SW1X 8PG.

For a fact sheet on anorexia, please write enclosing an SAE.

Women's Therapy Centre, 6 Manor Gardens, London N7 6LA. Telephone: 071 263 6200.

The centre runs courses and workshops, which often lead to the formation of self-help groups. They have also produced information booklets on bulimia and compulsive eating.

AUSTRALIA

Anorexia and Bulimia Nervosa Foundation of Victoria (Inc), 1513 High Street, Glen Iris 3146. Telephone: (03) 885 0318.

BANG (Bulimia and Anorexia Nervosa Group), Box 794, Nedlands, WA6009.

Queensland Association of Mental Health,
20 Balfour Street, New Farm, Queensland 400 J. Telephone: (07) 358 4988.

CANADA

BANA (Bulimia Anorexia Nervosa Association), c/o Psychological Services, University of Windsor, Ontario N9B 3P4. Telephone: (519) 253 7545. Hotline (519) 253 7421.

Eating Disorders Resource Centre of British Columbia, St Paul's Hospital, 1081 Burrard Street, Vancouver, British Columbia V6Z 1Y6.
Telephone: (604) 631 5313.

National Eating Disorders Information Centre, 200 Elizabeth Street, College Wing 1-328, Toronto.
Telephone: (416) 340 4156.

INDEX